CORVETTE
FIELD GUIDE

Jerry Heasley

1953 - Present

©2005 Jerry Heasley
Published by

kp books
An Imprint of F+W Publications

700 East State Street • Iola, WI 54990-0001
715-445-2214 • 888-457-2873

Our toll-free number to place an order or obtain
a free catalog is (800) 258-0929.

Library of Congress Catalog Number: 2004113669
ISBN: 0-87341-506-X

Designed by Brian Brogaard
Edited by Brian Earnest

Printed in the United States of America

CONTENTS

INTRODUCTION

"A Little Bitty Book"

It's all right to be little bitty; Alan Jackson sings. We agree. Our guide is little bitty- pocket-sized to carry in the field, to check out Corvettes.

In the little-bitty idiom, we have kept our comments pithy. Basically, this guide reveals Corvettes chronologically from 1953 through 2005, calling out germane details to differentiate one series from the next. The page on the right captions the image on the left, to keep it all simple.

Mostly, images depict stock Corvettes. Modifieds are part of the Corvette hobby, too. You encounter them in the field, so we have included a few.

We have also included famous factory show and experimental Corvettes, which spice up the hobby and get displayed at big shows around the country.

The book would be incomplete without "tuner" Vettes, such as built by Callaway Cars. Racecars are synonymous with Corvette, and they're here, too.

Many of the engines and cars chosen are "reference restorations," meaning concours correct.

As compact as this book is, the material inside encompasses 52 model years in bite-size chunks.

Yeah, it's all right to be little bitty—a little bitty house and a little bitty car—called Corvette.

DEDICATION

This book is dedicated to Chip Miller, who loved Corvettes. Most of us know Chip from his very popular "Corvettes At Carlisle" event, held annually each August in Carlisle, Pennsylvania.

At Bloomington Gold in June of 2004 near the Chevrolet Corvette display, about three months after Chip died, we spotted this sign with Chip's three word motto: "Life Is Good."

1953 WALDORF ASTORIA CORVETTE

This is the original GM Motorama show Corvette that debuted at the Waldorf-Astoria Hotel in New York City in January of 1953 to large crowds. Later, it became EX-122, an experimental development car to test the new Chevy V-8. The Original Blue Flame Six was pulled for a 265 V-8.

Exterior differences from stock include: door buttons, scoops on top of front fenders, hinged headlight grille doors, "CORVETTE" in script on the nose and deck lid, and special gold body spears on the side of each front fender.

This car is owned by largest Corvette dealer in world, Kerbeck Chevrolet, Atlantic City, New Jersey.

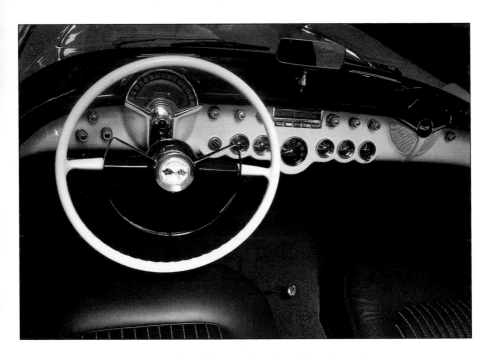

The cockpit was slightly different from production, including a large frame around the seats, and fiberglass with no vinyl "roll" that comes down the door panel and goes around the dash. Different arrangement of knobs and two extra knobs are found left and right of the dash. These opened and closed the cowl scoops on top of the front fenders.

The Kerbeck Brothers—George, Frank, and Charley—are good-natured enthusiasts who love people and love to share their priceless artifact at shows around the country.

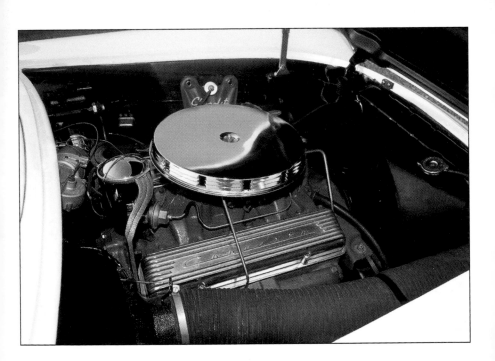

How would you restore this show car? Go back with a Blue Flame Six, as it was first built, or leave the 265? The Kerbecks left the 265, as tested as EX-122.

The V-8 was one of the first, or the first, V-8 ever installed in a Corvette. Chevrolet pulled the original test V-8 and replaced it with a fresh 265 before it was put up for sale in 1956.

Engineers made a notch in the frame to fit the V-8. It's the most historic notch in the Corvette kingdom.

1953 CORVETTE ROADSTER

This was considered the first "organic" American car design. It resembles a living thing— headlights are eyes, grille a mouth with teeth, emblem a nose.

It carried a radical new fiberglass body, the first by a major manufacturer.

Production began June 30, 1953 in the rear of a delivery garage in an old building on Van Slyke Avenue in Flint, Michigan.

The 1953s were all Polo White with Sportsman Red interiors and black soft tops.

There were only 300 copies built. These cars were in huge demand, and VIPs got preferential treatment. John Wayne owned one.

They were true roadsters with side curtains in place of roll-up windows, and a top that lifts off, rather than folding into a well. They were equipped with "Nerf" bumpers and pointed taillights. The exhaust exited through the fenders/bumpers for a jet airplane look.

The Blue Flame Six was based on the ubiquitous Chevy Stovebolt, a 105-horse utility inline six. It was hopped up with high-lift cam, solid lifters, and dual valve springs. The aluminum intake was fitted with three side-draft Carter YH carburetors. The result was the "Blue Flame Six" with 150 horsepower @ 150 rpm.

The 6-volt battery was easy to drain if the Carters were not adjusted and the choke first closed. Every Blue Flame Six was mated to two-speed Powerglide automatic. There were no manual versions.

1953 REVOLUTION ROADSTER

The '53 is so popular, enthusiasts build new cars from scratch.

A ground-up build, this Pugesek Motorsports' " '53" Corvette rod, dubbed the "Revolution Roadster," is a 2,300-lb. work of art. Its aftermarket body was painted PPG urethane Millennium Yellow. The frame is custom 2- x 3-inch suspended with tubular front upper and lower control arms and Aldan Eagle adjustable coil-over shocks.

The rear straight axle is suspended by custom four-link and Panhard rod. Custom Billet Specialties wheels mount Pirelli P-Zero Corsa tires. Steering is power rack-and-pinion.

The 1997 OBD II-controlled LT1 350-cubic inch crate engine supplies 350 horsepower and spins a 4L60-E automatic transmission and set of 3.43 rear cogs.

Inside, factory GM digital gauges fit into a hand-fabricated custom instrument panel

This vintage appearing rod has the comforts of a new Corvette, including keyless entry, intermittent wipers, alarm, GM 1996-vintage heating, ventilation, and air conditioning controls.

1954 CORVETTE ROADSTER

GM took a calculated risk and bet on the Corvette this year by building an assembly plant for the car in St. Louis. The plant had the capacity to build 10,000 cars per year.

Expanded colors included Sportsman Red, Black, and Pennant Blue, as seen here.

Production was 3,640, but about 1,100 remained unsold at end of the model year. Corvette was in jeopardy of being dropped.

The 1954 interior was carried over from 1953. Gauges were in easy view across the dash. The tach was in the center. The speedometer, in front of the driver, went to 140 mph. The Signal-Seeking radio cost $145.

Powerglide automatic was still the one transmission choice. The shifter was between the seats, at the driver's right hand.

1954 CORVETTE (REMOVABLE HARDTOP)

This is an unrestored "rare find" pulled from a garage in 2002 after 32 years in storage. It was bought new for $2,500 by Richard Hathaway. The sticker price was $3,000, which was a deal due to slow sales in 1954.

Hathaway ordered the hardtop from an aftermarket company in California because the factory did not yet offer the hardtop. Today, the body needs paint, but fiberglass does not rust.

Current owner Vic Lucarelli is the second owner of the car.

1954 CORVETTE MODIFIED

The original 1954 body remains stock on this car. Builders normally like a vintage appearance and do not alter these classic bodies. The body sits low to the ground and enhances the classic look.

Many customizers consider the original series 1953-55 original Roadster the best-looking Corvette of all time and thus the best type to modify.

The 1954 is the optimum car of this era to modify, due to higher production. Both the '53 and '55 are ultra rare by comparison.

Bob Devore at Centerline made four wheels from eight to get the offset right for a good fit. The wheels measure 18 inches up front and 17 in the rear.

This car is part of the Wayne Davis collection.

The original 1954 X-frame is easy to identify because it's painted red. The X-frame is highly modified to accept 1995 Corvette suspension, and powder-coated Inca Silver to pop out against the red 1954 frame.

The biggest job was cutting half shafts on the rear end to fit under wheel wells, which are modified to lay over the top of the A-frames.

Power comes from a 1968 Corvette L79, the 350-horse 327, pumped up with a pair of Edelbrock 600s. The dual quads give this '54 a 1950s performance look. Aesthetics are important on this car, where a silver and red theme prevail.

The polished aluminum Corvette valve covers are set off by red. Kirk Cunningham at Carriage Works built the custom air cleaner, also silver and red, with hidden fasteners. Allen-head screws secure the top from the bottom side.

The master cylinder is a work of art. Cunningham cut back a GM dual reservoir to fit in the stock '54 location under the hood. In keeping with the simple hot rod V-8, the distributor features stock dual points with a factory coil. This car contains no computer or high-tech electronics.

1955 CORVETTE ROADSTER

The 1955 model was again a carry-over from 1954 with minor changes. The big news was the arrival of the first V-8. The V-8 cars had a large, gold "V" on a small "v" in the Corvette logo on the front fenders.

Production was just 700 units, and attrition is believed to be very high for this model. About seven Blue Flame Six Corvettes were built.

Ford also introduced its Thunderbird sports car in 1955. Sales topped 16,000 and lines were drawn for a classic Ford/Chevy battle. The Corvette was here to stay.

The 265 delivered 195 horsepower and was standard with a three-speed manual or two-speed Powerglide automatic. A factory correct 265 has many unique details. There was no oil filter (until 1956 on the V-8). Special ignition shielding looks like a chrome tin can with a metal strap on top, covering the distributor and not extending down over the wires.

Due to the lack of sufficient ignition shielding, wires were metal-braided for the first time to suppress radio static— a trick not used until again the 1965 big block.

1955 CORVETTE EX-87

Duntov's "Test Mule" EX-87 was one of the experimental Corvettes Chevrolet used to develop both the 265 engine and the Corvette for high performance. Smokey Yunick built up the V-8 in his shop in Florida and Zora Arkus-Duntov drove EX-87 to a world record 163 mph in October of 1955.

The car had no hubcaps. Side exhausts exited in front of the rear tires. The headlights were covered. The headrest and extended rear fin were common on racing cars such as Jaguar and Mercedes in 1950s

This car is owned by Bob McDorman Chevrolet, Canal Winchester, Ohio.

1956 CORVETTE CONVERTIBLE

1956 saw the first major restyling of the Corvette. It had all-new body panels. The side cove was prominent and defines the Corvette look through 1962. The hood was upgraded with a pair of bulges running lengthwise.

Auxiliary hardtops were first offered by the factory this year. A total of 2,067 were ordered with this option. The soft top has power on 2,682 of 3,467 total Corvettes built for the model year.

The body changed from a roadster to a convertible, with roll-up windows and the top folding into rear well. Taillights were inset into rounded fenders. Exhaust pipes exited through fenders/bumpers for custom look.

Cascade Green was the least popular color in '56, and just 290 made. It is probably the most popular color today. Full wheel covers featured integral "two-bar" spinners.

This car is owned by Dick Mills.

All 1956s had V-8 engines—sixes were not available. The 210-hp 265 was standard and available for first time with manual transmission (three-speed).

The dual quad 265, seen here, was tuned to 225 horsepower with Powerglide and 240 horses with a three-speed manual. Dual point distributors were used for all but the standard 265.

This 265 has been restored to concours correct, down to original Carter dual fours, air cleaners, generator, and literally every little part and piece, including the 1956 window washer bag.

The instrument layout did not change appreciably for 1956. Gauges were still strung out across the dash, and the speedometer still went to 140 mph. An AM Signal-Seeking radio in this '56 reads "Wonderbar" in script that wasn't added until 1957. Very late-production 1956 Corvettes came with Wonderbar script.

This '56 was built on September 14, 1956, about two weeks before 1957 model year production began on October 1st.

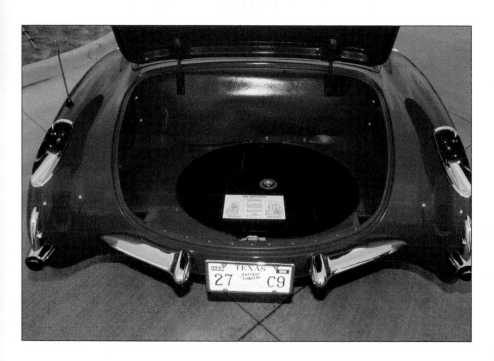

The trunk of the '56 is large for such a small sports car. The round piece of plywood covers a well molded to fit the spare tire. A trunk was an important part of a sports car's make-up in the classic years. A spare tire and jack were de rigueur for such vehicles.

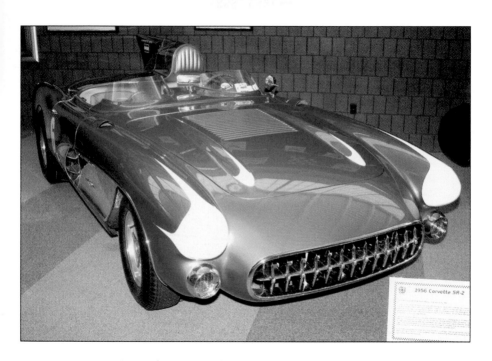

1956 Corvette SR-2

1956 CORVETTE SR-2

Racing definitely improved the Corvette. The factory raced prior to the AMA (American Manufacturers Association) ban in 1957, and racing continued to influence the company's decision making.

Zora Arkus-Duntov, named chief corvette engineer in 1955, knew racing prowess was the key to Corvette's survival in the race with Ford. Duntov eventually drove a '56 Corvette to a two-way average of 150.583 mph at Daytona's Flying Mile. And Dr. Dick Thompson won the SCCA championship in Corvette

GM Styling built this SR-2 for Jerry Earl, son of Harley Earl, GM's first design chief and the man that had convinced top executives they needed to build an inexpensive sports car for America. Features include a "low fin on the rear deck, air scoops in the side coves, twin rounded windscreens, larger front lamps under the headlights, and a grille section and nose extended substantially farther forward."

The car is now owned by Rich & Shar Mason of Carson City, Nevada.

1957 CORVETTE CONVERTIBLE

The 1957 Corvette body was a carry-over from 1956. Changes were concealed under the fiberglass skin.

Fuel injection was first introduced in 1957, the four-speed arrived, and a new Competition Handling Suspension, RPO 684, was available for racers. A positraction differential was used, and a quick steering adapter reduced lock-to-lock turns from 3.5 to 2.9.

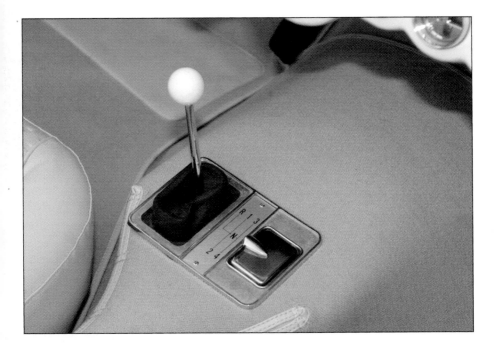

The stock 1957 four-speed featured a classic H-shift pattern. It was built by Borg-Warner. The white ball on the shift handle is factory stock for cars built later in the model year. Earlier cars came with chrome shift knobs.

1957 production was low at 664 units, due to late release of April/May time frame.

The 1957 283-cid engine was a 265 bored out 1/8th of an inch. The 220-hp four-barrel was standard. The dual-quad setup was rated at 245 hp with either the Powerglide or the manual transmission.

"Fuelie" became the nickname for a Corvette with fuel injection. The fuelie was available in four different horsepower ratings: 245, 250, 270, and 283. The 283 is praised as the first mass-produced engine to achieve 1 hp per cubic inch.

This fuelie rates 283 hp. Notice the shape and placement of the air filter element.

1957 CORVETTE CONVERTIBLE

Chip Miller helped define the gregarious, lend-a-hand attitude of Corvette people everywhere. Several months before he died (3/24/04), Miller sat down with his family and discussed donating one of his prized Corvettes to fight the rare blood disorder that he was battling.

This Aztec Copper '57 had a special mission—to kick off the fight against Amyloidosis.

At "Corvettes At Carlisle" in August of 2004, Chip's '57 brought $134,000 at auction. Donations can be made to the following:

The Chip Miller Charitable Foundation
1000 Bryn Mawr Road
Carlisle, Pa 17013-1588
www.carsatcarlisle.com
717-243-7855

1957 CORVETTE AIR-BOX FUELIE

There was still a hotter 1957 Corvette than the basic 283-hp fuelie—the Air-Box Fuelie. Just 43 were built with option code 579E.

Most (if not all) of the Air-Box Corvettes of 1957 also came with RPO 684, the heavy-duty racing suspension option.

These factory Corvettes were born to SCCA race. Dr. Dick Thompson took the SCCA B-production championship for the second year in a row.

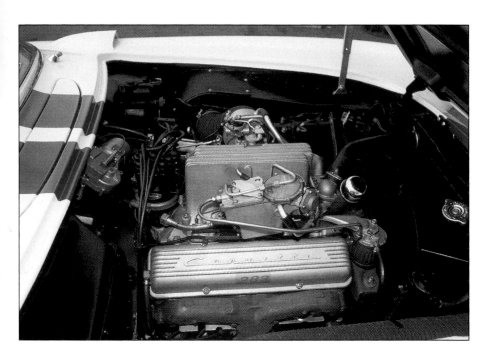

Enthusiasts call option 579E Corvettes "Air-Box" fuelies, for the unique fresh air intake under the hood. Notice the black flexible tube running to the air box on the passenger side of engine bay. This is the air box, which helps differentiate these cars from standard issue 1957 fuel-injected 283 engines.

Factory horsepower was still rated at 283.

The rare Air-Box Fuelie 'Vettes also came OEM (original equipment manufacture) with a mechanical tachometer mounted on top of the steering column, in easy view for the driver. The Roll bar is owner added, per SCCA rules. These cars were essentially built for amateur racers.

Sebring proved to be a racing milestone for Corvettes. The cars finished first and second in the GT class, 20 laps ahead of the closest competitors in a Mercedes.

If it hadn't done so before, the racing fraternity accepted the Corvette as a force to be reckoned with from then on.

1957 CORVETTE SS

This is the most legendary Corvette racecar of all time and the most valuable. It was born after Zora Arkus-Duntov and his crew set their sights on the 12-hour race at Sebring and built the Corvette SS. SS stands for "Super Spyder."

It weighed 1,850 lbs., had a 307-hp fuelie motor, tubular space frame and Dion rear suspension. Its mission was to destroy Mercedes, Ferrari, Jaguar, but the Corvette SS retired after 23 laps.

Ultimately, Detroit manufacturers supported the AMA ban on factory racing and the Corvette SS did not have a chance to develop in competition.

1958 CORVETTE CONVERTIBLE

The 1958 Corvette was re-styled with four headlights rimmed in chrome. A chrome stripe between each set of dual headlights ran the length of each fender. A scalloped hood was jazzed up with simulated louvers.

Three chrome strips were set in simulated side louvers in the front fenders. The wrap-around front and rear bumpers were larger. There were six exterior colors offered: Charcoal, Silver Blue, Regal Turquoise, Signet Red, Panama Yellow and Snowcrest White.

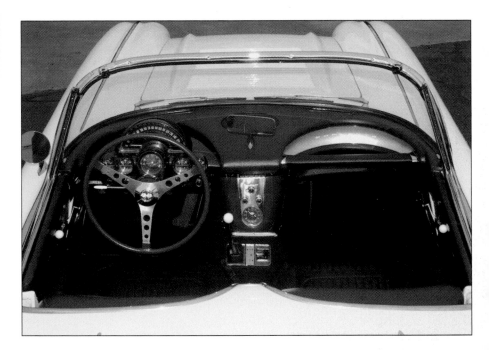

The interiors changed dramatically in 1958. 1958 gauges were clustered in easy view in front of driver. The large speedometer increased to 160 mph. The tachometer is much smaller, but well placed, and reads to 6000 rpm.

A grab bar was added to the passenger side. The console and factory seat belts were new. Previously, seat belts had been a dealer-installed option for 1956 and '57.

Options included a heater ($96.85), Signal-Seeking radio ($144.45), parking brake alarm ($5.40), power windows ($59.20) and windshield washer ($16.15).

The 230-hp four-barrel 283 was standard in 1958. The car had a top speed of about 103 mph and could do the quarter-mile in 17.3 seconds at 83 mph with a 4.11:1 rear axle.

Mike Wehrman restored this stock 230-hp 283 to concours condition. Mike's Vette fascination goes back to school days. "I bought a Corvette. I took it apart. My dad says, 'what the hell are you doing? That's a good car.'" Werhman recalled. "It was almost brand new. It took me a couple years to save enough money to get one. I was still in college, and ... I took it apart. Ever since I was a little kid I took things apart."

Thirty-five years later he's restored 15 Corvettes.

Fuelies came in 250-, 270- and 290-hp tunes. The air filter element, from 1957, was no longer used on the fuelies. The dual-quad 283 was offered in 245- and 270-hp tunes.

The finned valve covers featured "CORVETTE" script.

The base price of the 1958 'Vette was $3,591. It weighed 2,781 lbs. and a total of 9,168 were built.

1958 CORVETTE

The rear deck was adorned with twin chrome spears on the '58s.

Frequently, these chrome spears are missing on unrestored Corvettes. In the 1960s and 1970s they were pulled for a cleaner look. Today, these chrome spears are coveted and classic symbols of the era of chrome and fins.

The 1958 Corvette is well known for styling excesses. Some of these excesses were points of criticism in the car's heyday, and terms of endearment and glamour today.

Paint was upgraded from nitrocellulose lacquer to acrylic lacquer in 1958.

1958 CORVETTE NEWMAN CHASSIS

To make classic Corvettes more driveable, a number of aftermarket companies, such as Car Creations, owned by Paul Newman (not the actor) in Templeton, California, build hybrid chassis.

Here, Newman stands over a C1 (1953-62) frame, featuring the old X-member, modified to accept C4 (fourth generation, 1984-96) Corvette suspension components, including wheels and tires.

This '58 is a C1 body with a hybrid C1/C4 chassis. The body was also modified for 11-inch-wide ZR-1 wheels and P315/40/17 tires. Discs are found at all four corners and have aluminum calipers for maximum stopping power

Steering is rack and pinion. The forged aluminum suspension means less unsprung weight. Computer-designed suspension geometry provides optimum handling with modern radial tires.

This car is like a '58 for the 21st century.

A strange sight becoming more and more common on the Corvette scene is a late model engine under a C1 hood. This 1958 features a 1996 LT4 small block and a ZR six-speed transmission.

This great car is owned by Barry Long of Indianapolis.

1959 CORVETTE CONVERTIBLE

The 1959 body was similar to the 1958's, minus the simulated hood louvers. A bare-bones sports car was easily ordered for racing.

In 1959, Dick Kreps ordered this car with a 290-hp 283, four-speed, RPO 686 (metallic brakes) and positraction rear axle. To ready his '59 for the track, Kreps simply installed a roll bar, taped numbers on the doors, taped the headlights, and popped off the tiny hubcaps.

Gauges for the '59 were still clustered in front of the driver, but lenses were concave to reduce glare. All tachometers read to 7000 rpm in 100-rpm increments. They featured pale green, yellow and red zones for safe, caution and danger.

Small gauges flanked the tach and monitored fuel level, water temperature, battery charge and oil pressure.

1959 CORVETTE

This Roman Red with black interior '59, owned by famous Corvette collector Steve Hendrickson of Minnesota, is an unrestored "Survivor" and has attained "Benchmark" status. A Survivor, according to Bloomington Gold, needs to be original in three of the four categories: paint, interior, undercarriage and engine.

To rate Benchmark status, a Corvette must be original in all four of the same categories and also score high enough to win Bloomington Gold.

Hendrickson's '59 is original down to the Firestone 6.70-15s, which for may years were hermetically sealed for long-term storage. Hendrickson mounts them on the car for display. Although slightly cracked, they are serviceable.

Notice the width of the white sidewall. The factory mounted these very tires on this car in 1959.

Collectors get goosebumps looking at cars this original.

Under the hood of Hendrickson's Benchmark 1959 is the 270-hp dual-quad 283, which is essentially the fuelie motor without the sprinkler system. (Corvette-speak for fuel injection is "sprinkler system.")

The 270-hp 283 has the same cam and hard lifters (Corvette-speak for solid lifters) and compression ratio as the fuelie, but up top it's got the dual four WCFBs. They are intact and, like the rest of the car, completely original.

Cars such as this one provide a reference for concours restorations, to check what is stock.

1959 STING RAY RACER

Before the production Sting Ray (the spelling is different on the production car) of 1963, there was the Stingray racer, developed by Bill Mitchell, General Motors chief stylist and car enthusiast. Mitchell called the car a Stingray, not a Corvette, because Chevrolet officially had a ban on factory racing.

Mitchell bought one of the SS test cars from Zora Arkus-Duntov's 1956 Sebring program. Larry Shinoda, one of the stylists at GM, helped adapt the unique body to the Corvette SS chassis. The Stingray was Mitchell's personal project to go racing.

GM owns and shows this car.

The Sting Ray Racer's clamshell-style hood opened from the cowl forward for complete access to the engine. Corvette adopted the clamshell hood for the 1984 model, a quarter century later. Power came from a fuel-injected 283, which looks suspiciously newer than 1959 vintage.

The Sting Ray Racer has undergone numerous changes since 1959. In 1960, with drivers Dick Thompson and John Fitch, the Stingray Racer won the SCCA C-modified championship.

1953-60 CORVETTE HYBRID CHASSIS

Billy Dawson of Seguin, Texas, built his own frame from scratch for 1953-62 Corvettes. The frame accepts C4 (1984-96) Corvette suspension components and modern drive trains.

Dawson's company, "Corvette Corrections" of Seguin, Texas, operates out of a converted hangar where Dawson once built Hatz bi-planes

Here, Dawson sits in a rolling chassis, with the engine, transmission and rear end installed, ready for a classic body.

1960 CORVETTE

Corvette passed 10,000 sales for the 1960 model year, which was a first. The 1960 body style continued from 1959 and was the last year for grille teeth and rounded rear fenders.

Engine options were carried over from 1959. A 315-horse fuelie with aluminum heads was planned, but did not make production.

Dick Thompson drove Corvettes this year in the modified class, while Bob Johnson won B-production (SCCA) and Chuck Hall and Bill Fritts took the GT class at Sebring.

1960 CERV-I

CERV-1 was a rolling test-bed for engineering advances, or racing advances. According to GM, CERV stands for Chevrolet Engineering Research Vehicle. For Corvette enthusiasts, CERV stands for Chevrolet Engineering Racing Vehicle.

Duntov began designing CERV-I after his 1957 SS Sebring racecar was killed. The rear engine layout and tube-like body are reminiscent of an Indy racecar. Duntov would have loved to have raced CERV-I at Indy, but the GM corporate ban on racing prevented this attempt.

CERV I originally came with a fuel-injected 283-cubic inch engine. Duntov added a 377-cid aluminum small block, and lower, wider tires. Larry Shinoda also redesigned the body for better aerodynamics, as seen today.

Chevrolet donated the CERV-1 to the Briggs Cunningham Museum in Costa Mesa, California, in 1972. Today, CERV-1 resides in Mike Yager's "My Garage" collection in Effingham, Illinois.

1960 BRIGGS-CUNNINGHAM LEMANS CORVETTE

Chip Miller restored the Corvette of his dreams—this '60 model that actually won its GT class at LeMans, arguably the most prestigious race in the world.

Chip finally displayed his dream 'Vette at his own Corvette show, "Corvettes At Carlisle," during Labor Day weekend, 2003.

Once upon a time, Corvette racecars were prepared from assembly line units, as was the case with the trio of 1960 models Briggs-Cunningham built to race in 1960. Sometime in the 1960s, somebody, yet unknown, converted this LeMans-winning Corvette back to a street car.

Kevin Mackay, celebrated for his meticulous restorations of great racing Corvette ghosts of the past, actually tracked down the long-lost LeMans winner. He restored the car in his shop, Corvette Repair, Valley Stream, New York.

Racing at LeMans in 1960 was a much more quaint venture than it is today. Notice the two red lights and the bungee strap holding down the rear deck lid on this car. This is the view the rest of the GT field had of this Corvette when it crossed the finished line at LeMans.

"I graduated from high school in 1960. It was during college that I really discovered the Corvettes of the 1958-60 vintage," Miller recalled. "I just liked them. They were brand new Corvettes of my youth. In 1962, when I graduated from college, I bought a '60 Corvette. It was my first Corvette."

1961 CORVETTE

The body shell on the 1961 Corvette was a carry-over from 1960. The heavy grille teeth were replaced with an argent silver-colored grid. Headlamp rims were painted body color.

Sateen Silver cars like this were the rarest, with only 747 built. Total production for the model year was 10,939 cars. About 52 percent of those cars came with a detachable hardtop, and almost two-thirds had a four-speed manual transmission.

A re-styled rear end was influenced by the Sting Ray Racer. Four taillights were seen instead of two. Exhausts exit below the body, not through the rear fenders. Crisp lines replace the rounded look.

The design was a predecessor to the Sting Ray coming in 1963 and added more room to the trunk. The rear emblem had a spun silver background with the crossed flags over a "V" design and the words "Chevrolet Corvette."

Wheel covers over steel rims remained standard in 1961. Custom wheels had not yet made their way onto the scene. Integral two-bar spinners featured "Chevrolet Corvette" script and crossed flags logo.

It was the last year for wide whitewalls. Wheels measured 15 x 5.5 inches. Option code 276 gave buyers an upgrade to half-inch wider wheels with small hubcaps in the center, instead of a full wheel cover.

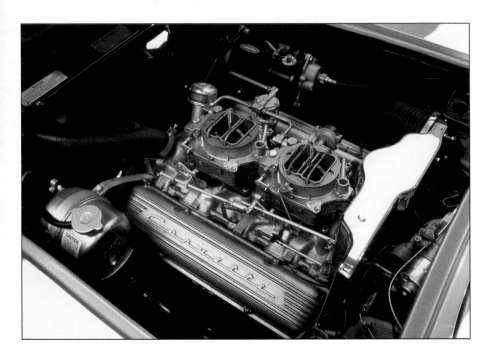

1961 was the last year for the 283 and the last year for dual-quad carburetors. The dual-quad was offered in either 245- and 270-horse versions.

The standard engine was a 230-hp/283-cid four-barrel. Fuelies had 275 or 315 horses.

1961 CORVETTE MAKO SHARK

This car is the most famous show Corvette ever made. It was originally named the Shark, then renamed the Mako Shark in 1965.

The vehicle was styled by Larry Shinoda and inspired by a real Mako Shark Bill Mitchell caught off the coast of Florida. The paint scheme matches a mounted and stuffed shark hung on the wall in the GM Styling Center. The top is an iridescent blue, fading into white along the lower body.

The body is a Sting Ray, but with an elongated nose and gaping mouth like a shark.

The Mako Shark is currently powered by all-aluminum ZL1 427. The block is black, and heads and intake are aluminum. It originally had 327 hp. It's now reputed to have 650 hp.

The air cleaner and valve covers have saw tooth edges reminiscent of shark teeth.

This showpiece resides in the care of GM in the General Motors Design Center, not far from Mitchell's old office.

1962 CORVETTE

The 1962 Corvettes were the last of the "Straight Axles" (named for solid rear axle), or first-generation Corvettes, now known as "C1" for Corvette, generation one.

It was also the last year, until 2005, for exposed headlights. The headlights were painted, not rimmed in chrome, and the mesh grille was blacked out, giving the car more of a performance look.

Popular Honduras Maroon adds an *American Graffiti* coolness to this '62.

1962 was the first year for the 327, which was a bored and stroked 283.

In Corvette-speak, Steve Hendrickson says: "My Honduras Maroon/black interior '62 is a hard-lifter 340-horse/four-speed with two tops, heat and music, and a 3.55 Posi. It's got the big valves like the fuelie and the same cam profile with solids and 11.0.1 compression, all without the maintenance and temperament of the more sophisticated fuel delivery system."

Four-barrel 327s were standard with 250 horses, with 300- and 340-hp options available for more performance-oriented buyers. With the extra cubes, the fuelie was rated at 360 hp, making it the strongest "Straight Axle" ever.

The side cove was no longer rimmed with chrome in 1962. The cove was painted the body color, not a contrasting color.

A single louver with a grid replaced the three chrome spears in the simulated front louvers.

Narrow whitewalls were a first. The original tires are seen here.

1962 GULF OIL RACE CAR

This high-performance 'Vette was Raced by Dr. Dick Thompson to the SCCA, A-production national championship in 1962. Later, it was returned to street condition and sold, but its race heritage was hidden for years.

This remarkable car was bought by Michael Ernst of San Diego in 1980. The ragged roadster was a heavy-brake and suspension 'Vette. RPO 687 was a $333.60 option that outfitted these cars with heavy-duty brakes and suspension parts. Just 246 such cars were built in 1962.

Both the 1962 Gulf team cars were painted white with blue stripes in Briggs Cunningham tradition, with blue coves.

In the 1960s, many racecars were returned to the everyday use and disguised as street cars. A title search revealed this '62 had once been a graduation present for a high school senior and had been stolen and recovered at least once.

1962 "OLD SCHOOL"

Old School is in session. The course is Backyard Engineering. The year was 1968. Bob Shetler bought this '62 Corvette for $375. The body was a wreck. He visited the junkyard many times.

The brake system is from an S-10 pickup truck. The steering is from a '72 Corvette. The tilt steering column is '75 Chevy van. The cruise control is off an '84 Corvette. The five-speed is from an '88 Pontiac. The hood scoop is off a '67 Corvette.

Bob Shetler said of his "Old School" build: "We would work on it through the years, I would find something in a junkyard I thought would fit and I'd make it fit … The V-8 is a tuned-port 350. Don't ask me the year."

Practically since dinosaurs roamed the earth, 'Vette people have dropped hotter V-8s into their Straight Axles. They'd do most anything to go faster and handle better—blowers, turbos, nitrous, fatter wheels and tires, subframe connectors, digger gears, Posi, you name it.

Chrome is good. More chrome is better.

Bob Shetler trailers his '62 to events with a crew. They wear black Polo style shirts stitched discretely with "Xtreme Vette." The entire crew loves the old style. Mike Burger, the painter, stored this Straight Axle in his garage for most of the last 20 years.

"We grew up together," Shelter says.

1962 "NEW SCHOOL"

On the outside, this '62 looks vintage. Underneath and inside, it's a C5 (1997-2004 Corvette).

Owner Ben McMurry of Fayetteville, Georgia, cut out the 1962 floorboard and firewall, and cut the trunk area to make the body fit.

Fire up this hybrid Vette and basically, you're driving a C5. The outside door latches, inside door latches, and all the mechanisms that make the door work are all C5.

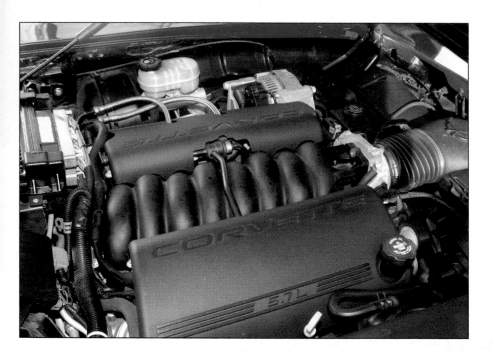

Power on Bob McMurry's C5 '62 comes from a computer-controlled LS1 that was stock in the 1997-2004 Corvette. The LS1 develops 345 horsepower, a net figure more powerful than the top-rated fuelie in 1962.

The LS1 fits like it was made for the '62 engine bay. Even the exhausts route out the back of the '62 like a C5, but the bezels are from a 1972 Corvette.

Perhaps the biggest contrast in this custom car is its '62 cockpit fitted with a C5 dash and seats.

The interior has all the modern conveniences—cruise control, power mirrors, power door locks, power windows, tilt wheel, Bose radio, heating and air conditioning controls—literally everything from the C5.

"I just had to trim the pad," McMurry said. "And then I had to put a little dash cap on it cause it didn't fit all the way up."

1963 CORVETTE SPORT COUPE

1963 marked the start of the second generation, the C2. More than a new design, the 1963 'Vette was a revolution. This was Bill Mitchell's all-new Corvette, complete with an independent rear suspension and all-new coupe body.

The coupe featured a radical fastback roofline with a center piece dividing the glass for an exotic, almost show car appearance.

The coupe became known as the "split-window." The 1963-67 generation cars have become known as "Mid-Year" cars.

Another sensation in 1963 was option P48, for cast aluminum knock-off wheels. Knock-off means that, in true racecar fashion, there are no lug nuts. The wheels come off by knocking the ears protruding from the center hub, which loosens a large central lug.

Unfortunately, aluminum wheels had to be delayed due to problems with porosity, which often caused the air to leak and the tires to flatten.

The wheels seen here are true 1963 knock-offs, as denoted by the rare two-bar spinners. Apparently, some sets of knock-off wheels were sold.

1963 CORVETTE Z06

The Z06 originated from a simple option code from 1963. It was the code for the "Special Performance Package."

Just 199 Z06's were built in 1963 for coupes and convertibles. Early cars went to established racers like Mickey Thompson. The package retailed for $1,818.45 for the "split-window" coupe.

The Z06 package included sintered metallic brake linings, plus larger finned brakes drums, vented backing plates and cooling fans in the drums. Air was ducted to the linings through "elephant ears" seen here.

These heavy-duty binders are drums, not disc brakes. Brake linings had to warm up first to work. Once they warmed up, they worked great, were good for the race and very durable.

1963 CORVETTE, "BIG TANK"

N03 was the option code for the fabled "Big Tank," a 36-gallon fuel tank for the coupe. The tank took up most of area behind seats. Just 63 cars were built with N03, which was intended for the Z06, but optional for all coupes.

This setup gave racers the ability to stay on track longer between fill-ups and was intended to make the cars more competitive in long-distance events, such as Daytona.

1963 L84 FUELIE

The L84 code called for the 360-horse/327-cid fuelie. The L84 was mandatory with the Z06, which required a four-speed Muncie (no longer a Borg-Warner) and positraction rear end.

The Z06 was a very expensive car in 1963– more than $4,500 if you threw in the $202 big tank.

A new dual-cockpit body style individualized the driver and passenger sides in 1963. The instrument panel featured round gauges, deeply recessed. A 160-mph speedometer and 7000-rpm tachometer were the same size, evenly spaced in front of the driver.

Part of the roof swung away with door for easy access.

1963 CORVETTE 327

Engines in 1963 were carry-overs from 1962. The four-barrels were 250, 300 and 340 horsepower. The fuelie was the 360-horse.

New alpha-numeric option codes were easier to say and created identifiable names. L84, for example, denoted the 360-horse fuelie. L76 was the 340-hp with solids. Enthusiasts call out their engines by option code and the names stick.

Z06 would become a legend as it won races and enthusiasts repeated the name over and over.

1963 BUNKIE KNUDSEN CORVETTE STYLING TWIN

In the 1960s, executives had "styling" cars built for their own use and for friends or VIPs. Werner Meier (Master Works, Madison Heights, Michigan) has restored many of the styling Corvettes of the 1960s and is the acknowledged expert on these cars.

Meier restored this flashy '63 convertible originally built for GM President William "Bunkie" Knudsen. The most complicated part of the restoration was fabricating the side exhausts, mufflers and muffler covers.

Technically, Knudsen's '63 is not a styling car because it was built by Chevrolet Engineering. However, it is a twin to a styling car.

The car is now part of the Bob McDorman Collection in Canal Winchester, Ohio.

1963 HARLEY EARL STYLING CORVETTE CONVERTIBLE

Harley Earl was the GM design chief who convinced top executives they needed to build an inexpensive sports car for America. He was no longer GM Chief Of Design (Bill Mitchell was) when the styling department at Chevrolet built this 1963 convertible for him.

According to Werner Meier, this convertible was built for Earl and delivered to his home in Florida. It features custom chrome side pipes and a white racing "stinger" stripe running over the top.

Inside Harley Earl's car, unique rally instrumentation featured an exotic accelerometer and a 24-hour rally clock on the passenger side.

The flat-faced gauges on the driver's side are also special, laid out on a white background. Non-stock metal floor grilles protect the carpet and add show car look. Most styling cars had these.

The seats featured vertical white stripes. The door panels are also unique. Executives could not only order such cars for themselves, but they could order them for celebrities and many got them, including actress Elizabeth Taylor and General Curtis LeMay.

This car is now part of the Bob McDorman Collection in Canal Winchester, Ohio.

1963 CORVETTE GRAND SPORT

The 1963 Corvette Grand Sport was Duntov's answer to the racing Cobra, Carroll Shelby's aluminum-bodied sports car that had a 1,000-lb. weight advantage over the production Corvette.

The Grand Sport was exotic, built on a ladder-type frame with Sting Ray suspension, and weighed less than 2,000 lbs. It carried an experimental, fuel-injected, 550-hp/377-cid V-8 that featured an aluminum block and two sparkplugs per cylinder.

The factory would not support racing, so Duntov sold the five Grand Sports to privateers, including Grady Davis, Dick Doane, Jim Hall and John Mecom. Later, Roger Penske and George Wintersteen cut the tops off of two of the coupes and made them into roadsters.

At Nassau, in December, 1963, a trio of Grand Sports beat the Cobras in the unlimited class. This #003 GS, driven by Roger Penske and Jim Hall as part of the John Mecom Racing Team, was given the name "Cobra Eater."

It is now owned by Tom Armstrong of Issaquah, Washington.

1964 CORVETTE COUPE

New one-piece glass was used for the rear window in 1964 as the Corvette coupe was no longer the "Split-Window."

New slotted wheel disc covers were used. This car wears the original size 6.70 x 15 whitewall tires.

The rear quarter louvers were restyled this year. Right side ducts become functional, and air was ducted through the cab via electric motor.

Coupe production dropped to 8,304 cars.

1964 CORVETTE CONVERTIBLE

Corvette production increased to 13,925 cars for 1964, of which 7,023 had the auxiliary hardtop. Only 919 convertibles had air conditioning.

Convertible and coupes lost a pair of decorative grids in the top of the hood. Rocker panels were bolder looking.

Engines for the year were carry-overs, but the fuelie was upped to 375 hp and the L76 grew to 365 hp. Knock-off wheels were available, but featured three-bar spinners instead of two, as in 1963.

1964 CORVETTE STYLING CAR

This car was modified at Design Staff for Ozzie Olson, an industrialist who prepared Indy cars called Olsonite Specials. It has custom side exhausts, lower front fenders modified to a flat surface, no scallops, and features capital letters of "STINGRAY." It also has a total of six taillights—three per side.

This example was restored by Werner Meier at Masterworks Automotive Services in Madison Heights, Michigan, where he and a number of serious gear heads and craftsmen spend their days restoring these treasures to their former glory.

The car is part of the Bob McDorman Collection, Canal Winchester, Ohio.

1964 WORLD'S FAIR CORVETTE

This Chevrolet styling Corvette was built for display at the 1964 World's Fair in New York. Its showy side pipes and the fuel injection unit rising out of a hole in the hood are the most obvious show car features. Its egg crate grille was fabricated out of aluminum plates. It was built with disc brakes, which were not available in 1964. It carries a 375-hp/327-cid fuelie engine.

Incredibly, this car is unrestored. The Candyapple Red lacquer still glows.

Two simulated brake vents appear in the top of the rear deck. They were not functional, but similar to vents used on Duntov's exotic Stingray racer.

The back end featured six taillights—three per side—that were much wider and larger than stock.

The Corvette emblem this Stingray carries is unique.

Today, the car resides in Mike Yager's "My Garage" collection in Effingham, Illinois.

The interior of the World's Fair Corvette remains original and unrestored. It gives the car a definite nostalgia feel and provides a glimpse into the past.

The door panels feature three sequential flashing lights set against a bright background. High-backed bucket seats feature special leather trim.

Carpeting is cut pile instead of the original loop. The weather-stripping is red. The carpets are protected with metal floor grilles.

Overall, the interior is worn, but in excellent condition, glowing through an iridescent patina of age.

1964 MISS MAKO

Miss Mako was a personalized, female replica of the more macho Mako Shark. It featured "Miss Mako" script and shark emblems in real silver on front quarters.

Stainless steel pipes were bent, welded and polished. The rear end was re-worked and features three taillights per side.

The hood is not as large as original Mako Shark and the front grille resembles a shark mouth with teeth.

Miss Mako was restored by Dave Secaur at "Final Finish" in Branford, Connecticut. The car is owned and by Joan Spoerndle, who saw the original 1961 Mako Shark and tried unsuccessfully to buy the car.

1964 PRO STREET CORVETTE CONVERTIBLE

"Pro Street" means out-of-bounds performance on the street. Corvettes have seen their share of these builds, especially with the least collectible of the mid-year series –the '64.

The 540-cubic inch big block cranks out more than 600 horsepower. A Perry Competition shifter controls the two-speed Powerglide. Underneath is a narrowed Dana 60 with four-link and Koni coilovers.

The front bumper was pulled, and a tall cowl induction hood scoop added. White urethane paint with pearl, accented with candy stripes of silver, magenta and sapphire blue was topped with clearcoat.

1965 CORVETTE SPORT COUPE

The 1965 coupe was the first Corvette with four-wheel disc brakes standard. Drum brakes were available as a delete credit option, but just 316 were made. The '65 was also the last Corvette with fuel injection until 1982.

New side louvers in the front fenders were functional vents. Cars with the new 396-cid motor had a "power blister" hood scoop. Knock-off wheels were painted dark gray between the fins.

Total coupe production was 8,186 cars.

1965 CORVETTE CONVERTIBLE

The '65s had new black horizontal grille bars inside a bright surround. The big-block hood had exclusive bulge in the center, with simulated louvers on each side. A power antenna was added and was standard.

Sidepipes, officially option N14 and called the "side mount exhaust system," were often ordered with the big block, as seen here.

Convertible production was 15,376 cars.

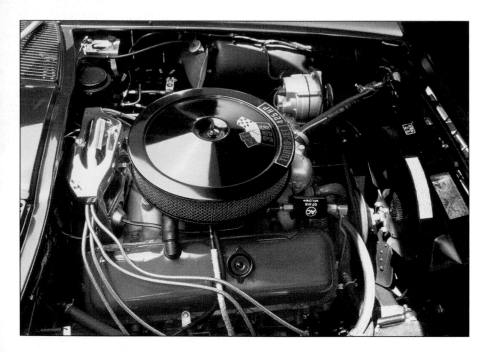

1965 CORVETTE 396

The big-block 396, aka the Mark IV, arrived in the spring of 1965. This engine, at $293 extra, was more bang for the buck and sounded the death knell for fuel injection, at $538. The 396 was rated at 425 hp.

Just 2,157 big blocks, option code L78, were built in a half model year production run. They were not available with air conditioning, and required a transistor ignition.

Stock wires were metal braided for radio suppression.

Overspray of orange engine paint on the aluminum intake is a factory procedure.

This concours-restored Milano Maroon convertible features AM/FM radio, teak wheel (but no "Tele"), a four-speed, and vinyl upholstery (not optional leather). The gauges were redesigned with flat, black faces. The disc brakes on this car do not have the power assist. The Comfort and Convenience Group features back-up lights and a day/nite mirror.

1966 CORVETTE COUPE

Zora Arkus-Duntov, chief Corvette engineer, poses here with a brand new 1966 Corvette coupe.

The bulge in the hood indicates this car has a big block. The Corvette script on the hood and driver's side was added for '66. Roof vents were eliminated this year.

Coupe production for 1966 was 9,958 cars.

1966 CORVETTE CONVERTIBLE

This Rally Red Corvette was the last 1966 convertible built. It has a 425-hp/427-cid four-speed with a M21 Muncie transmission, and 4.11 Posi rear end. The optional F41 suspension pins the power to the ground. J56 special heavy-duty brakes came with a unique master cylinder and had to be ordered with J50 power brakes.

Deleting the heater (in the cold Midwest) showed the obvious bent the first owner had toward performance. Sidepipes provided the sound, as the radio was also deleted. The center cone on the knock-off wheels has a dull finish.

Convertible production was 17,762 for 1966.

1966 CORVETTE 427/425

The 427-cubic inch motor is a bored and stroked 396. This L72 feature was first rated at 450 hp at start of the year, then changed to 425 hp. These 427 cars were also known Mark IIs.

The big-block heads were nicknamed "porcupine" due to the seemingly random placement of valve stems sprouting from beneath the rocker covers.

The L36 option 427 motor rated 390 horsepower. Small-block engines were base 300-horse 327s and optional 350-horse 327s—both four-barrels. The fuelie was dropped this year.

1966 CORVETTE SCCA A-PRODUCTION ROAD RACER

Vintage racecars like this '66 coupe, driven by legendary Corvette driver Bob Johnson (Marietta, Ohio), are very hot collectibles today.

Kevin McKay of Corvette Repair in Valley Stream, New York, found and restored this '66 coupe that Johnson raced at Daytona in 1967 at the American Road Race Of Champions.

This car took first place in 1966 at Cumberland Airport in May, Mid-Ohio (the Johnny Appleseed 150) in August, and Marlboro in September. It also took second in the IRP National in October.

Owner Doug Bergen named his '66 big block "8-Ball"—the position so many race drivers found themselves behind on the track.

Racecar owner Doug Bergen factory ordered this racecar from the order form, receiving a brand-new '66 Corvette with the 425-hp/427-cid with an M-22 four-speed and 12-bolt Posi rear end. The 427 looks close to stock. The air cleaner decal reads 625 horsepower.

Bob Johnson began racing and winning with the stock 425-horse engine, slightly improved with a modified Holley four-barrel. In the second race, the 427 spun a bearing and Bergen called Yenko Sportscars in Canonsburg, Pennsylvania, to buy a new big block. The 427 was pretty much an L88 build, which was the coming thing for Chevrolet racers.

In the 1960s, SCCA rules were amazingly easy to follow to go racing: a little wider tire, no fender mods. You could change brake pads, but had to leave on the stock calipers. Bergen didn't even change out the gas tank for a fuel cell. A roll bar was mandatory. Bergen modified the hood by replacing the latch with one hood pin and pulling the gills. Bergen also installed a racing seat and two of the racing Raydot mirrors on the fenders. He pulled the bumpers to save weight.

Corvette aficionados like to reunite the racecar owners and drivers with their old rides. It's like they're part of the original equipment. In 2000, at the National Corvette Museum in Bowling Green, Kentucky, famous Corvette driver Bob Johnson (right) and owner Doug Bergen meet up with their '66 SCCA A-production road racing coupe, decked out like it was in the 1960s Bob Johnson should be very familiar to Corvette aficionados.

One way to think of Bob is he was the Dr. Dick Thompson or the John Fitch of his era, the late 1960s and early to mid-1970s. Bergen took a chance on Johnson, a beginning racer at 40 years of age. Some people say life begins at 40. Racers say it begins at 140—mph.

1967 CORVETTE CONVERTIBLE

1967 marked the last year for the C3, or Mid-Year design of 1963-67. The hood script emblems and fender flags were removed, otherwise the convertible and coupe were carry-overs from 1966.

Five slots defined the working louvers in the front fenders. The hood scoop was called the "stinger" and was for big-blocks only.

Knock-off wheels were now a cast-aluminum "Bolt-On" style using lugs hidden by the large center cap.

A triangle-shaped air cleaner assembly denotes "Tri-Power." This term refers to a trio of two barrel Holley carburetors, offered on the 427 big block in two tunes—the L68 (400 horse) and L71 (435 horse), seen here.

The L68 Tri-Power was the choice for owners who wanted to order air conditioning—not available on the L71.

L89 was the aluminum head option for the L71. Horsepower was still 435. Of the 3,754 L71s built, only16 had the L89.

1967 CORVETTE "435" CONVERTIBLE

This was the L71-powered 1967 'Vette. Among its more subtle nuances was the removal of the grab bar in front of the passenger, and the relocation of the emergency brake handle from under the dash to the console between the seats. The seats were redesigned and the radio was installed vertically.

A total of 20,182 of 22,940 Corvettes came with four-speed manual, divided between the standard M20 (9,157), the close-ratio M21 (11,015)), and the close-ratio, heavy-duty M22 (20).

1967 CORVETTE L88

The L88 engine was factory rated at 430 horsepower—five less than the L71. Somewhere above 5000 revs, the L88 peaked at 530 horses. Some sources say 620.

An obvious trick by the factory was the "IT" engine suffix code, seen in the white tag on the valve cover face. This engine, essentially, was "it," meaning the highest performance, not the 435.

The air cleaner was not restrictive. Resistance to fire was supplied by the wire mesh screen. There was no emission equipment. The road draft tube was visible on the passenger side.

Neither radio nor heater were available with L88. Chevrolet did not want to see these cars on the street. They were meant for racing.

Just 20 L88 Corvettes were built for 1967, in both coupe and convertible.

Duntov's plan was to keep the option hush-hush. The factory was out of racing, but the L88 gave racers a chance to do battle. Tony DeLorenzo raced this convertible.

To put the story in fairy tale form, in 1967, Chevrolet was the feudal landholder (manufacturer) and Tony DeLorenzo was the mounted man-at arms (racer) giving service as a favorite son. Raised in the palace (his father was an executive at Chevrolet), DeLorenzo was a zealous competitor on the field of battle (SCCA amateur road racing tracks). It was his pleasure to use his high-born training in service to his sovereign, who wore the honorable bow tie.

1967 "BODY DROP"

Corvettes are body-on-frame, meaning the body lifts off of a platform-type frame. Naturally, complete restorations are body-off-frame.

This 1967 small block has been restored to concours condition, including color codes and various ink stampings on the frame and chassis.

Roger Gibson, a professional restorer from Scott City, Missouri, is under the body as the chassis is rolled into position for the body drop. Scary for most restorers, the job is done here with a set of $100 camper jacks, the normal assortment of tools and a body mount kit. Gibson does the body drop with the doors open, which stabilizes the body and positions the edges of the camper jack close to the front fenders.

1967 CORVETTE COUPE

As highly acclaimed and popular as the coupe was through the 1963-1967 (Mid-Year) era, sales continued to lag behind convertibles by a healthy margin. The tally was 8,504 to 14,436 for the 1967 model year.

This Sunfire Yellow coupe was one of 16 built with the L89 aluminum head option on the L71, which was 427 Tri-Power in the 435-horse tune. This car has the Rally wheels, which were standard equipment and did not cost extra in 1967.

1967 CORVETTE SMALL-BLOCK 327

The 327 small block was a carry-over from 1966. As before, the base 327 had 300 hp. Exactly 6,375 Corvettes came with the optional 350-hp 327, seen here restored to No. 1 condition. Finned aluminum valve covers are cast with Corvette script.

Notice the chrome shielding on the ignition, which since 1964 had been optional with K66 (transistor). The intake is aluminum. The engine is painted Chevrolet orange.

1967 CORVETTE CONVERTIBLE WITH AUXILIARY HARDTOP

One reason for the popularity of the 1967 convertible was the auxiliary hardtop. Presto, the convertible became a hardtop.

James Shelley of Albany, Kentucky, restored this Marina Blue '67 to concours shape. Shelly likes to brag that his '67 has no power steering or power brakes, but contends that the car doesn't need these extras with the small block engine up front.

Big-block 1967s might have bragging rights in acceleration, but small block fans will say 350-horse 327 is balanced much better.

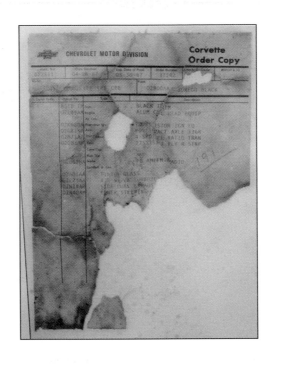

CORVETTE GAS TANK STICKER

Here is the often spoken about, but seldom seen, "gas tank sticker." Glued atop the gas tank, these factory build sheets normally suffer the ravages of weather until after decades they deteriorate. These weathered scraps authenticate factory equipment and are a vital part of factory paperwork on a vintage Corvette.

A gas tank sticker such as this one is worth its weight in gold, and a lot more in this instance, considering the data revealed, including the aluminum cylinder heads and the 435-horse 427.

The poor condition of the sticker makes it all the more authentic. Of course, there's no way to restore such a sticker. Owners save these stickers in their safety deposit boxes at the bank and make copies for display.

MANTA RAY

Just as there was a Sting Ray racer in 1959 that foretold the future look of the '63 Corvette, in the mid-1960s there was a Mako Shark I, a Mako Shark II and a Manta Ray that foretold the third-generation Corvette that would debut in 1968.

Actually, the Mako I was not a running model. The Mako Shark II was a running model and in 1969 was remodeled and renamed the Manta Ray, seen here.

As hot-looking as the Mid-Year Corvettes were, the next generation held even more promise of a futuristic design with radical elements like a chopped roof, a hinged roof panel for entry, a periscope in lieu of a rearview mirrors, a louvered rear window, and even pop-up rear brake flaps.

The rear of the Manta Ray reveals exotic pop-up brake flaps, shown here in the up position. Imagine these flaps opening for every stop. They would surely warn drivers in the rear.

The "tunnel backlite" features curved buttresses. These items were much straighter on the production '68 Corvette coupe.

The ZL1 badge is a late addition to the original show car, as was the ZL1 big-block under the hood. The Manta Ray script on the top right rear deck is next to a stylized badge in the image of a shark.

1968 CORVETTE SPORT COUPE

The 1968 cars were the first of the C3, or third-generation, Corvette. Collectors refer to these 1968-1982 models as "Shark" cars.

The '68 excited the Corvette community with its Coke-bottle shape, Kamm-back tail, and arching fenders. It carried the third-generation Corvette for the next 15 years.

The fastback was replaced by coupe with tunnel-back featuring roof pillars, looking suspiciously similar to the 1964 Ferrari GTO. Overall, the Coke-bottle shape was a production version of the radical Mako Shark II and Manta Ray of the mid-1960s.

The T-tops, when removed, gave the coupe the open-air feeling of a convertible. Coupes came with new shoulder belts.

1968 CORVETTE CONVERTIBLE

Convertibles outsold coupes 18,630 to 9,936 in 1968. Chassis were carry-overs, with some refinements, from the previous generation C2s.

Engines were also carry-overs. The M40 Turbo Hydra-Matic, a three-speed automatic, replaced the two-speed Powerglide. The battery was relocated to the area behind the seats. Exterior door handles were replaced with door buttons.

The 1968 models, although enthusiastically received, did have teething problems with quality control. Restored 1968s are uncommon.

1968 CORVETTE ZL1 RACECAR

This car was restored to perfection by the world's preeminent Corvette racecar restorer, Kevin Mackay of "Corvette Repair" in Valley Stream, New York.

It was fabricated in the early 1970s using Greenwood body panels and endurance raced in 1972 and 1973 in GT class (Sebring, Daytona, LeMans) by the team of John Greenwood and Dickie Smothers, the famous comedian. The car was sponsored by B.F. Goodrich and used to test the first radial tires which would appear on the Corvette in 1973.

The "stars and stripes" theme was common on Corvette racecars of the era. This showstopper was powered by the illustrious all-aluminum ZL1 big-block 427.

1969 CORVETTE COUPE

Stingray (one word) was found in script on the front fenders above new side vents on the 1969 Corvettes. Exterior door "handles' changed from a button to a rectangular chrome plate that pushes in.

The 350 replaced the 327, and the base motor was rated at 300 horses. A 350-hp (L46) was optional. The 427s also returned, plus the all-aluminum 427 (ZL1).

This Daytona Yellow coupe is a small block. You can tell by the un-scooped standard hood.

1969 ZL1 CORVETTE SPORT COUPE

For many muscle car and Corvette fans, this car is the Holy Grail. Only two of these cars were ever built.

The ZL1 was the option code for the all-aluminum 427. Black stripes were unique to Corvette with the ZL1 engine.

In 1990, federal agents seized this ZL1 in a cocaine bust. The Government Service Administration (GSA) auctioned the car for the United States Marshals on October 11, 1991, in Florida. Bidding started slowly at $50,000. Auctioneer Terri Goveia had asked for a half million dollars to open. Roger Judski of Maitland, Florida, was the winning bidder at $300,000. His plan is to keep the car for life.

The ZL1 Corvette was an L88 in aluminum clothing (block and heads and intake), which subtracted 100 lbs. from the front end.

Why just two were built remains a mystery. Expense was one aspect—it cost more than $4,700 for the engine option alone, or more than the cost of an entire car in 1969. The L88 was $1,032 extra for the same outrageous output of horsepower and torque.

Off the showroom floor, the ZL1 was capable of sub-11-second quarter-mile ETs, according to a story from Karl Ludvigsen's book "Corvette: America's Star Spangled Sports Car."

Roger Judski, the owner of this ZL1 for the last 13 years, says the factory rating was 430 horsepower, but unofficially, they were rated at 560.

1969 CORVETTE CONVERTIBLE 427

This 1969 Corvette is a big block, as denoted by the scooped hood, which also carries 427 scripted badges on each side. This Tuxedo Black convertible is an L89. The L89 option placed aluminum heads on the L71 (Tri-Power, 435-hp/427-cid) and increased in popularity from 16 in 1967, to 624 in 1968, to 390 in 1969 as buyers became more aware.

1969 was the last year for the L89.

This car is part of the Milton Robson collection.

1969 CORVETTE CONVERTIBLE L88

The scooped hood indicates this 1969 has a big block. The extra rise in the fiberglass denotes the L88 option, which had the 427-cid/430-hp V-8.

L88 production increased from 20 units in 1967 to 80 in 1968 and 116 in 1969. 1969 was also the last year for L88.

This car is part of the Steve Hendrickson collection.

1969 BALDWIN-MOTION PHASE III GT CORVETTE

"Baldwin" refers to Baldwin Chevrolet in Baldwin, New York. "Motion" refers to Motion Performance, a speed shop owned by Joel Rosen in Long Island, New York.

Rosen built his "Fantastic Five" supercars in Impala, Chevelle, Camaro, Corvette and Nova.

The ultimate Corvette was the Phase III GT, guaranteed to run the quarter-mile under 12 seconds.

The 427-cid big block, originally a 435-horse Tri-Power 427, is tuned for over 500 horsepower.

1970 CORVETTE COUPE

The 1970 Corvette body was a carry-over with a few minor tweaks—fender flares, new egg-crate front fender louvers, and a new front grille with square mesh pattern. Under the hood, the 427-cid V-8 was stroked to a 454.

Coupe sales passed convertible sales for first time— 10,668 to 6,648. Possibly, the T-tops were a factor. With the tops removed, the coupe had the flavor of a true convertible.

Production dropped to lowest its total (17,316) since 1962 due to the extended 1969 model year. 1970 production did not start until January of 1970

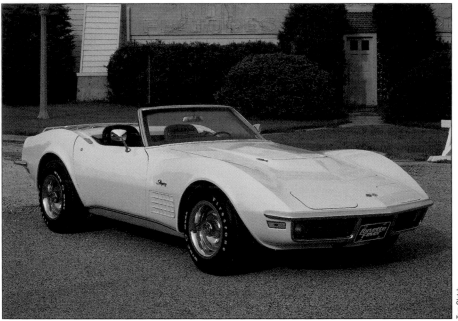

1970 CORVETTE CONVERTIBLE

This was the year of the first ZR1 "Special Purpose Engine Package," highlighted by a new 370-hp 350-cid (LT1 option) and M22 four-speed. Only 25 of these cars were built.

There were only four engine choices:

300-horse 350 (standard)
350-horse 350 (L46)
370-horse 350 (LT1)
390-horse 454 (LS5)

LS7, a 460-horse 454 was canceled, leaving no "hot" 454. The LS7 had an iron block with aluminum heads. Also developed was an LT-2 with an aluminum block and aluminum heads. Neither made production.

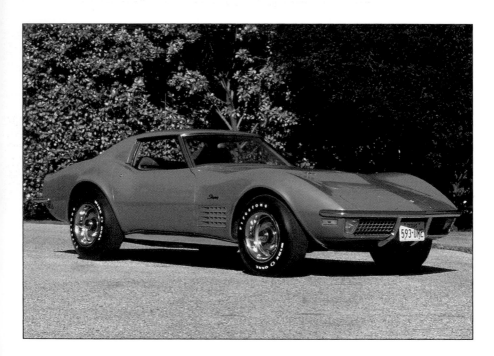

1971 CORVETTE COUPE

The 1971 body style was not a carry-over from the previous year. The LS6, a 425-hp 454, was added to the lineup. The base 350 dropped 30 horsepower to 270. The LT1 350 dropped 40 horsepower to 330. The LS5 dropped 25 horses to 365.

The automatic transmission was very popular with Turbo-Hydra-Matic production of 10,060, almost 50 percent of the run. The coupe outsold the convertible 14,680 to 7,121.

1971 LS6 ENGINE

"De-proliferation" continued in 1971 to lower engine and transmission combinations. The LS6 was a 425-horse version of the 427 that produced 390 lbs.-ft. of net torque at 3600 rpm. It had five main bearings, hydraulic lifters, and a Holley four-barrel. All Corvette engines ran on regular fuel.

The LS7 (465 hp) was nixed due to its ultra-high compression ratio. Engines were gradually getting smaller compression ratios so they ran better on lower-octane gas.

1971 CORVETTE ZR2

For 1971, the ZR1 was joined by the ZR2. The ZR2 was a performance and handling package based on the LS6 big block. The ZR1, which returned from 1970, was a performance handling package based on the LT1 small block.

Just 12 ZR2s were built, compared to eight ZR1s for 1971.

This concours-condition Brands Hatch Green coupe is from the Otis Chandler collection.

1972 CORVETTE SPORT COUPE

The 1972 body was a carry-over—including the design of fender vents. The 1971s and 72s had the same grille. It was the last year for front and rear chrome bumpers, and also the last year for the removable rear window.

Factory hood stripes identify this 1972 coupe as having the LT1 engine option.

Enthusiasts call this Corvette the LT1, the engine option code, which Chevrolet integrates into the hood stripe.

1972 LT1 ENGINE

Horsepower ratings changed from SAE gross to SAE "net" in 1972. The gross figures are higher and do not subtract parasitic losses from accessories. The LT1 was rated at 255 hp, down from the 330 rating of 1971.

The LS6 454 engine was dropped. The LS5 454 was rated at 270 horsepower, down from a 390 rating of 1971. 1972 was the one year the solid-lifter, high-revving LT1 could be ordered with air conditioning.

1972 CORVETTE CONVERTIBLE

The 1972 convertible was also a carry-over design. The ragtop continued to decline in popularity with 6,508 convertibles produced compared to 20,496 coupes.

Air conditioning was becoming more common—17,011 had air of 27,004 total cars produced.

The ZR1 special purpose package on the LT1 for road racing was available on the coupe and convertible. Only 20 were made. The ZR2, a special purpose package on the 454 big block for road racing, was dropped.

1973 CORVETTE SPORT COUPE

A new front end appeared in 1973 with body-color urethane over new bumpers designed to withstand 5-mph impact. The rear bumpers remained chrome, and were not yet affected by government standards. The 1973 cars were the only Corvettes to use chrome and urethane bumpers.

Radial tires were first available this year. Front fender louvers were redesigned. Back windows were not removable.

A total of 25,521 coupes were made.

1973 "CORVETTE SUMMER" CORVETTE

"Corvette Summer" was an MGM movie from 1978. Mark Hamil (made famous in "Star Wars"), played Kenneth W. Dantley, Jr., who customized this wrecked Corvette in high school auto shop class. The Corvette used in the movie has achieved near cult status.

Among its features were a boat tail front end with dual quad headlights, a clam shell hood, side pipes, custom paint and Superior Industries wheels.

Today, "Corvette Summer" cars have a worldwide following. Copies have been made, and more than one movie car exists.

This example is from Mike Yager's "My Garage Collection."

1974 CORVETTE SPORT COUPE

This amazing unrestored 1974 has only 902 original miles.

Rear bumpers were designed to withstand federal 5-mph impact standards on the 1974 Corvettes. New two-piece, body-color urethane rear bumper covers were used. A new sloping rear deck was integrated with the urethane bumper cover. The tail was redesigned.

The tires for this '74 are almost extinct. Firestone recalled its "Steel Radial 500" series because the steel belts separated.

New Gymkana suspension (FE7) appeared on 1,905 cars. The Z07 off-road brake and suspension package for L82 and LS4 went on 47 cars. This required the four-speed M21 option.

Total production increased to 37,502 (32,028 coupes and 5,774 convertibles).

Shoulder belts integrated with the lap belts for 1974. Seat belt "interlock" prevented starting the car if the driver and passenger were not buckled in. Under the hood was a black re-set button to disconnect the interlock mechanism. Most of these systems were deactivated or no longer survive

Virtually every Corvette has power steering in 1974—35,944 of 37,502 built. A total of 19,959 Corvettes had the Custom Interior, which included leather seats. Air conditioning went on 29,397 cars. Turbo-Hydra-Matic was the overwhelming transmission choice with 25,146 units.

The base 1974 engine was the L48 195-horse/350-cid mill seen here in mint original condition, unrestored with 902 miles.

The L82 was the hot 350 with 250 horsepower. 1974 was the last year for the big block. The LS4 454 was rated at 270 horsepower. It was also the last year without catalytic converters, and the last year for true dual exhausts. Each muffler had a resonator.

The Corvette scored IMSA GT-class wins at Daytona and Talladega, and SCCA national championships in A- and B-production, and B-Stock Solo II.

1975 CORVETTE CONVERTIBLE

There was no rush to buy the last open Corvette. Of the 38,465 total 1975 Corvettes built, just 4,629 were convertibles. Convertible sales slowed so much, Chevrolet decided to drop the body style after the model year was over.

Bumpers were slightly changed and had simulated pads, front and rear. Not visible were structural upgrades underneath

L82 script was attached to the hood, as seen on this Orange Flame '75 convertible.

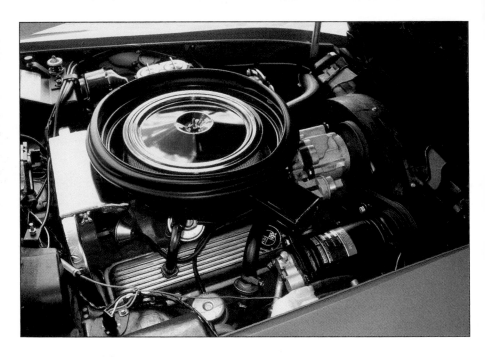

1975 CORVETTE L82 ENGINE

The standard 1975 engine was the 160-horse 350. The one optional engine was L82, a 350 with 205 horsepower seen here. A total of 2,372 L82 'Vettes were made this year.

This original engine is concours correct. The smog pump at the top frequently got tossed on these motors. Air conditioning went on 31,914 units. It was the first year of catalytic converter.

The Z07 "Off Road Suspension and Brake Package" was available on the L82 only, at a cost of $4,000. It included the FE2 gymkhana suspension plus heavy-duty front and rear power brakes. Just 144 buyers anted up for this option.

Zora Arkus-Duntov, Corvette's first and only chief engineer, retired and was replaced by David McLellan.

John Greenwood won the SCCA Trans Am title in a Corvette.

1976 CORVETTE SPORT COUPE

1976 was the first time the coupe was the one and only body style for a Corvette. To add strength and improve shielding from exhaust system heat, a partial steel under-body replaced fiberglass. New Kelsey-Hayes aluminum wheels installed on 6,253 cars, seen here.

A new one-piece nameplate was placed on the rear, between the twin-unit taillights.

Both V-8s offered this year had four-barrel carburetors.

Production took another jump, up over 7,000 units to 46,668.

1976 CORVETTE, ENGINE

Engines took on a totally different look when Chevrolet inducted air up front "over-the-radiator," rather than the cowl as in the past.

The base 1976 350, seen here, increased 15 horsepower over the previous year to 180. This concours-correct, reference original motor reveals the factory clutter of hoses and wires.

The L82 was the one engine upgrade, and at 210 hp rated 5 more horsepower than the previous year.

1977 CORVETTE SPORT COUPE

T-tops for these cars fit in the luggage and roof panel rack. A total of 16,860 of these Corvettes were built.

Speed Control was new. It required automatic transmission and was installed on 29,161 cars. Leather seats became standard in place of vinyl.

Chevy Orange engine paint changed to blue. Headlight-dimming, wipers and washers were controlled by a steering column stalk The engine lineup carried over from 1976.

On March 15, 1977, the 500,000th Corvette, a white coupe with red interior, was produced in St. Louis.

1978 INDY PACE CAR CORVETTE

The first re-design since 1968 came in 1978, but the cars were not a new generation—they were still C3. There were 25th anniversary emblems on all cars.

The Corvette paced Indianapolis 500 for first time, and 300 Indy pace car replicas were planned, the same as produced in 1953. Chevy upped production to one per dealer, 6,502 were built, to meet demand.

Pace cars are their own series, identified in VIN, called "Limited Edition Corvette." The package consisted of front and rear spoilers, unique silver interior with lightweight, high-back bucket seats, white letter tires on alloy wheels, lift-off glass canopy roof panels, and special decals.

A special "Silver Anniversary" package went on 15,283 cars. It included a two-tone silver paint job plus aluminum wheels and sport mirrors.

The fastback returned for the first time since 1967.

1978 GREENWOOD-KIT CORVETTE

John Greenwood catapulted to fame when, in 1971, he co-drove his red/white/blue Corvette to victory at the 12 Hours of Sebring with the famous comedian Dick Smothers. His 'Vettes stood out with their low, wide bodies, looking almost like caricatures of the stock Corvette.

Greenwood built 43 total custom street Corvettes from 1975 to 1981 in five different styles: the Sebring GT, Sportwagon, Turbo GT, Daytona, and GTO. These cars were copied in kit form, as seen here.

The owner, John Zandy, believes the body panels for his Greenwood kit were built by ACI. Greenwood Corvettes, then, fall into three main categories, the authentic racing cars, one of the 43 Greenwood street customs built by Greenwood, and one of the kits, as seen here.

1979 CORVETTE SPORT COUPE

Bodies for the 1979s were the same as the previous year, with upgrades from Limited Edition pace car-high-back bucket seats, and removable roof panels with mirror glass finish. Front and rear spoilers from the 1978 pace car were optional.

Production topped 50,000 (53,807) for first time. Three price increases pushed the base price over $10,000 for first time.

The most popular color was Black, followed by Classic White, Silver, and Corvette Red, seen here.

Engines for 1979 were the same as 1978 with slightly improved power ratings. The base L48 was up 10 horsepower to 195.

The L82, seen here, was up 5 hp to 225. A dual-snorkel air cleaner gave it a performance look.

The L82 shown here is an unrestored original with low miles and is unchanged from new.

1980 CORVETTE SPORT COUPE

A new front bumper cover integrated the lower air dam for a cleaner appearance and a more aggressive grille on the 1980 Corvettes. Front fenders came with functional, black air louvers. A new rear bumper cover integrated the spoiler into the deck, eliminating the optional spoiler of 1979.

The coupe lost about 250 lbs. due to more liberal use of aluminum (differential housing and supports, intake manifold) and other advances, such as lighter roof panels.

The standard engine in California Corvettes was the 305-cid code LG4, which complied with that state's tough emissions standards. Other states got the 190-horse 350 as the base engine.

The L82 returned for its final year with 230 horsepower. This L82 coupe features the N90 option aluminum wheels. Notice the L82 script on the front fenders, also new for 1980.

A strange sight on 1980 'Vettes was the 85-mph speedometer—a new federal requirement. With 55-mph speed limits imposed after the fuel crisis of 1973, 85 mph apparently seemed high enough.

Otherwise, the cockpit remained sporty. The speedometer and tachometer were easily visible through a three-spoke steering wheel.

This car is an automatic, mandatory with the L82 this year. The four-speed was not available with the L82, although a few might have been produced early in the model year.

1981 CORVETTE

The body for 1981 was a carry-over from 1980. The year also marked the first time since 1954 that only one engine was offered, a 190-hp 350. The L82 and 305 California-smogger were dropped.

One cosmetic change saw the Corvette crossed flags and bow tie badges edged in black instead of chrome, as in 1980.

Corvette production moved in the middle of the model year to a new assembly plant in Bowling Green, Kentucky.

Many enthusiasts modify their early 1980s Corvettes, such as Mel Thomason did with this '81 coupe. Corvette did offer a charcoal/silver, upper/lower body paint for 1981. This red/silver T-top is similar, but not a knock-off of the '81. This color scheme is more like the '78 Pace Car, with the lower silver paint flowing up and over the wheel wells.

1982 CORVETTE "COLLECTOR EDITION"

All 1982 Corvettes were built in Bowling Green, Kentucky. It was the last year for the long-in-the-tooth C3, which dated back to 1968. The chassis went back to 1963 and the C2.

1982 was also the last year for 8-track tape players.

The "Collector Edition" was the first Corvette to retail for more than $20,000. It was easy to identify with its unique silver-beige paint, featuring body side decals that faded from dark at the front to light at the rear. The alloy wheels were designed to resemble original knock-off wheels from '63.

The fixed rear window was replaced by a lift-up glass hatch, another Corvette first.

1982 CORVETTE CROSS-FIRE ENGINE

The new 1982 "Cross-Fire" was the first fuel injection system for the Corvette since 1965. The system had a pair of injectors that sprayed fuel into the throttle body. The engine looked trick with large oval air cleaner assembly, angled to make it similar in appearance to a cross ram induction on a dual-quad 1969 Z/28 Camaro.

The new injection system increased horsepower to 200. Manual transmission was not certified for use with this engine. These cars were available with automatic only.

1983 CORVETTE

The '83 Corvette is a ghost. Chevrolet was late with the introduction and decided to just skip the entire model year and introduce the all-new Corvette as an '84.

Even though 1983s were not sold to the public, Chevrolet did build 1983 models, which the press drove at Riverside Raceway in December of 1983.

This author attended those previews and test drove an '83 for *Super Stock & Drag Illustrated* magazine and spun a red '83 at over 100 mph on a decreasing-radius turn, was black flagged and ruined all four tires.

Occasionally, the National Corvette Museum in Bowling Green, Kentucky, will put an '83 on display.

The 350 Cross-Fire was a carry-over from 1982. Horsepower was rated at 205. Spark plugs were easy to change with the fender wells out of the way. The clamshell hood would help Corvette to fast pit stops in racing. Plus, it was just a blast to open to show off what was under the hood of your new Corvette.

The Z51 was a Performance Handling Package that had directional alloy wheels (16 x 8.5 in front and 16. x 9.5 in rear), heavy-duty front and rear springs, shocks, stabilizer bars and bushings, quicker steering ratio, and an engine oil cooler.

Critics were turned off by digital gauges. Speed and rpms were illustrated graphically by liquid crystal displays.

The cushion on the panel in front of the passenger was the remnant of a still-born passive restraint system, which the government dropped in the new Reagan administration.

Late in the model year, automatic was joined by a manual four-speed built by Doug Nash. The novel four-speed was called the "4 ┼ 3" because each of the first three gears had an overdrive to improve fuel economy.

A total of 51,547 cars were built.

1985 CORVETTE

Word had spread that the ride was far too harsh on the '84 Corvette, so a softened suspension was given to the standard and Z51 cars. The two exterior changes were the "TUNED PORT INJECTION" on the fender molding and straight tailpipes.

Otherwise, the changes to the car were under the skin, ranging from 8 1/2-inch ring gears for manual transmissions, to bolder instrument cluster graphics, glass roof panels with more solar screening, a new heavy-duty cooling package, and 9 1/2-inch wheels front and rear on the Z51 option.

The smooth nose of the car was decorated by nothing but retractable headlights.

The 1985 cars had the new TPI (tuned port injection) 350, and horsepower jumped from 205 to 230.

A box-shaped plenum was replaced with eight aluminum runners tuned to produce more power at lower rpm, in the same manner, Chevrolet claimed, of the "tall stacks mounted atop many race engines."

The Bosch TPI injection system mounted the fuel injectors in the manifold base plate. Air flowed from the front of the radiator through a Bosch hot wire mass airflow sensor and into the plenum. It was distributed through the ports and into combustion chambers.

1986 CORVETTE CONVERTIBLE

The '86 ragtop was the first convertible 'Vette since 1975. A new third brake lamp appeared on top of the rear tail light board on the convertible, and above the rear hatch hinge on the coupe.

ABS (anti-lock braking) introduced. Wheel centers were natural finish instead of black. A new vehicle anti-theft system (VATS) placed sensors in the doors and hatch to trigger an alarm and imbedded small pellets in the ignition keys for positive identification.

Aluminum heads were standard on the TPI 350 engine. A four-speed overdrive had an up-shift indicator light on the instrument cluster to optimize fuel economy.

1987 CORVETTE CONVERTIBLE

Coupe and convertible bodies remained the same this year as they had been the previous year. Argent gray paint in the wheel centers replaced the natural finish.

The TPI 350 increased 10 horsepower to 240 courtesy of lower-friction roller valve lifters.

The Z52 Sport Handling Package (for coupe and convertible) was a softer version of the Z51 Performance Handling Package (coupe only).

1987 CORVETTE CALLAWAY TWIN TURBO

Checking option code B2K on the Corvette order form netted an "off-campus" engine option for $19,995. The Bowling Green Assembly shipped a new Corvette to Callaway Cars in Old Lyme, Connecticut, for a twin turbo treatment on a 350, producing 345 hp and 465 lbs.-ft. of torque.

An aero body, as seen here, was available. Just 184 B2K Corvettes were ordered: 121 coupes and 63 convertibles.

1988 CORVETTE 35TH ANNIVERSARY COUPE

1988 was the last year for the Doug Nash "4 + 3" manual transmission. It was also a year that was largely unchanged in the styling department.

New standard wheels (16 x 8.5 inches) featured six slots. The 350 TPI had 240 hp, except coupes with the 3.07 axle. They were rated slightly lower at 235 hp.

The B2K optional engine increased to 385 horsepower with a price tag of $25,895.

The 35th Anniversary package was made for the coupe. These cars were white with black roof bow, white door handles, white body side moldings, white painted wheels and center cap, 35th anniversary badges on the front fenders. They had white seat trim, a 35th anniversary badge embroidered on the seat, white steering wheel leather on the rim and center, a white console lid, white door trim panel and armrests, white door trim panel and armrests, a transparent roof panel and more. A total of 2,050 were built.

1988 CORVETTE CHALLENGE

Chevrolet launched its own showroom stock race series this year called The Corvette Challenge. It used identically prepared C4 Corvettes.

Engines were built in Flint, then sealed and shipped to Bowling Green Assembly for installation. Final assembly, including roll cages, was done at Protofab in Wixom, Michigan.

Driver talent determined the winners in these races. Here, Corvette Challenge cars battle in Dallas in May of 1988. Stu Hayner was the inaugural champion driver.

Just 56 of these cars were built.

1989 CORVETTE SPORT COUPE

A new six-speed ZF manual transmission appeared with CAGS (computer-aided gear selection). A solenoid forced the shifter into fourth gear under a light throttle (for better fuel economy), instead of letting the driver shift from first into second. The solenoid didn't engage under hard throttle. Most enthusiasts disengaged the CAGS.

Selective Ride Control offered coupe drivers a choice of Touring, Sport or Competition settings.

There was a new fiberglass removable hardtop for convertibles. A new standard wheel had 12 slots, the same as the 1988 wheel with the Z51 and Z52 options.

1989 was the last year for the Corvette Challenge. Sixty Challenge cars were built.

A total of 16,663 coupes were built, plus 9,749 convertibles for a grand total of 26,412 cars.

1990 ZR-1

The ZR-1 super car burst onto the scene in 1990, powered by the LT5 DOHC (dual overhead cam) V-8. The ZR-1 was 1 inch longer and 3 inches wider than the standard coupe. The wider body required new doors, rear quarters, rockers, rear fascia and rear upper panel for wider rear wheels (17 x 11 inches) and larger P315/35ZR-17 tires

There was no convertible and no automatics. All the cars were six-speed coupes.

The ZR-1 had a convex rear end with rectangular tail lamps, compared to a concave back with round lights on the standard 1990 model coupe. The ZR-1 also has rectangular exhaust outlets.

Exactly 3,049 ZR-1s were built for 1990 at a cost of $27,016 over the base price ($31,979) of the coupe.

The ZR-1 came with the LT5, which is the RPO code for the exotic, DOHC V-8. The engine itself is often mistakenly called the ZR-1. The ZR1, however, is the entire "Special Performance Package."

LT5 displacement was 350 cubic inches, the same as the standard L98 small block. The LT5, however, was a new design developed by Lotus and Chevrolet and built at Mercury Marine in Stillwater, Oklahoma.

Four overhead camshafts and 32 valves (four per cylinder) made the valve train exotic and high revving. An all-aluminum engine, the LT5 pumped out 375 horsepower at 5800 rpm. The rev limiter was set at 7200 rpm from the factory, shutting off fuel to avoid damage to accessory drives. The LT5 held 12 quarts of oil.

1990 CORVETTE INTERIOR

The 1990 'Vettes had a new instrument cluster with analog and digital gauges. The console, door trim and steering wheel were redesigned. Switches and controls had raised symbols that were both easy to see and feel. Power door and window switches were relocated to the door. The windshield wiper switch was moved to the turn signal stalk. The driver's-side air bag standard.

The valet switch on the console of the ZR-1 needed to be turned on to unleash the full power of the LT5.

1991 CORVETTE SPORT COUPE

The 1991 cars were distinguishable by their new front fascia with wraparound park/turn lamps. The standard coupe and convertible featured body-color body-side moldings and new gill panels. The wheels were also a new design, as seen here, but the same size (17 x 9.5) as 1990.

The B2K option for the Callaway Twin-Turbo was in its final year. Just 62 were sold at a cost of $33,000—for the engine option alone, or higher than the $31,683 for the LT5 engine option. Corvette captured the manufacturer's title in the World Challenge for the second straight year.

Production totaled 14,967 coupes (including 2,044 ZR-1s) and 5,672 convertibles.

1991 CORVETTE ZR-1

The first major restyle since 1984 added ZR-1-type exterior appointments to the Corvette coupe and convertible. The 1991 models shared the wide rear fascia and four rectangular taillights.

Because the ZR-1 had 11-inch-wide rear wheels, the doors and rear body panels were still unique. The ZR-1 also mounted a center stop lamp in the roof, while coupes and convertibles mounted this brake light in the top center of the rear taillight board. A ZR-1 badge appeared on the rear fascia.

1991 CALLAWAY SPEEDSTER

The Speedster was the ultimate Callaway of the 1990-96 era. Just 11 were built in this exotic body style. One Speedster had a top.

They were powered by a 403-hp, twin-turbocharged 350. Two cars had ZR-1 engines. Twin scoops in the hood fed twin intercoolers.

The cars had a top speed 177 mph and did 0-to-60 mph in 4.1 seconds.

They carried a staggering base price of $131,000.

1 MILLIONTH CORVETTE

On July 2, 1992, the 1 millionth Corvette, a white 1991 convertible with red interior, seen here, rolled off the Bowling Green Corvette assembly line. Chevrolet flew members of the press to Nashville and they drove the Corvette north to Bowling Green to celebrate and write stories. Zora Arkus-Duntov drove the Corvette through the paper barrier as Chevy brass clapped and yelled. It was a grand affair.

The National Corvette Museum was under construction less than a mile from the assembly plant. Everybody took a tour of the soon-to-open, $35 million facility. Hundreds of people signed the underside of the millionth Corvette. The car now resides in the museum in Bowling Green.

1992 CORVETTE ZR-1

The 1992 ZR-1 was a twin to the '91 with a few minor exceptions. Two large rectangular exhaust tips replaced the four slightly squared tips, and new ZR-1 badges appeared above the front fender vents.

Production dipped dramatically from 2,044 cars in 1991 to 502 units in 1992. There were probably several reasons for this drop-off. Dodge's V10-powered Viper roadster stole some of Corvette's thunder, and Corvette was no longer America's only sports car. The ZR-1 cost $31,683 plus the base price of the coupe, which was $33,635, for a total of $65,328, not counting any other options and shipping charges.

Chevrolet would have to up the ante with an exotic new body or lower the price to put the ZR-1 back in the sales picture.

1992 CORVETTE LT1

The new 1992 LTI 350 had reverse-flow cooling, meaning the heads were cooled first, then the block. Synthetic oil was another improvement.

Chevrolet named the new option LT1 after the famous solid lifter Corvette small blocks of 1970-72. The 300-hp rating was the highest "net" horsepower for a small block in Chevy history.

Chevrolet claimed the LT1 equaled or exceeded existing world-class V-8 engine standards for mass, size, fuel consumption, emissions and cold starting.

1992 CORVETTE CONVERTIBLE

1992 was another year of carry-over styling for the Corvette, in both the convertible and coupe.

A new traction-control system was a joint Chevy/Bosch effort, and named Acceleration Slip Regulation (ASR). ASR took the slip out of tires, which was good for driving in rain, ice and snow, but disabled classic tire burnouts. A switch on the instrument panel turned off the ASR, which engaged with each ignition.

New Goodyear Eagle GS-C high-performance tires (directional) replaced the Eagle ZR Gatorbacks.

1993 CORVETTE "40TH ANNIVERSARY"

In the midst of a year of very few changes in looks, Corvette celebrated its 40th anniversary with a "40th Anniversary Package," available on coupes, convertibles (seen here) and the ZR-1. The package included an exclusive Ruby Red exterior and interior with color-keyed wheel centers, headrest embroidery and bright emblems on the hood, deck and side-gills. Corvettes with leather seats also got the 40th anniversary logo.

Production was very healthy at 6,492 cars. More than half the production run of the 502 ZR-1s were Ruby Reds (245).

1993 CORVETTE ZR-1

Dodge's Viper RT/10 had 400 horsepower, so Corvette's LT5 engine in the ZR-1 was upgraded from 375 to 405 horsepower through modifications to the heads and valve train. The bottom end was also beefed up with four-bolt mains.

The coupe and convertible were largely carry-overs from 1993. The LT1 was also carry-over with 300 horsepower.

All Corvettes came with Passive Keyless Entry (PKE). A transmitter inside the key opened the doors in close proximity to the vehicle.

ZR-1 production dropped from 502 to 448 for the model year. Overall production was 15,898 coupe and 5,692 convertibles, for a 21,590 total.

The redesigned 1994 interior featured a new two-spoke wheel, and new gauges with white graphics that turned tangerine at night. There were also new door trim panels with storage bins. A passenger side air bag and knee bolster were added. The driver's power window featured an "express down" function.

Seats were either standard reclining buckets or optional articulated Sport seats, both designed for easier entry and exit. Cloth was dropped and all seats are made of leather.

The tire jack was mounted in an individual storage compartment behind the passenger seat.

1994 CORVETTE SPORT COUPE

The changes for 1994 were all underneath the fiberglass skin. The LT1 engine, although still rated 300 horsepower, improved with new sequential electronic fuel injection (SFI).

A much more desirable mass airflow sensor (MAF) replaced the old speed-density system. The MAF was more conducive to engine mods. R-134 refrigerant replaced the old style freon in the air-conditioning system.

Optional Goodyear "Extended Mobility" tires could run without air for up to 50 miles. They required the low-pressure tire warning option.

1994 CORVETTE CONVERTIBLE

Externally, things remained pretty much status quo on the 1994 Corvettes. The backlight and heated glass were new on the convertible. The top still folded into its well automatically.

For better ride quality, engineers lowered spring rates with the optional Selective Ride Control. In conjunction, they reduced the recommended tire pressure to 30 psi.

The 4L60-E, four-speed automatic overdrive transmission, standard equipment on LT1-powered coupes and convertibles, was redesigned for smoother shifting.

1994 CORVETTE ZR-1

The ZR-1's new five-spoke, non-directional aluminum wheels measured 17 x 9.5 inches up front and 17 x 11 inches in the back—the same size as 1993. The ZR-1 label was found on the wheels.

Goodyear Eagle GS-C steel-belted, directional, asymmetrical tires were P275/40ZR-17 in the front and P315/35ZR-17 in the rear, requiring larger fenders than the coupe and convertible.

ZR-1 production was identical to 1993 at 448 units. Chevrolet limited production to the same figure as the previous year. The end of the ZR-1 was in sight.

1995 CORVETTE SPORT COUPE

The 1995 coupe had restyled fender "gills" in the air vents. Otherwise, the '95 models resemble the '94s in coupe, convertible and ZR-1. The heavy-duty brake option, part of the ZR-1 previously, became standard on all models.

Optional Sport Seats had "French" seam stitching for more strength. The seat-back lever and bezel were color-keyed to the seats. The instrument panel had automatic transmission fluid temperature display.

A new spare tire delete option was offered for cars with run-flat tires.

1995 CORVETTE CONVERTIBLE

Corvette again paced the seventh running of the Indianapolis 500 in 1995. Chevrolet built a Dark Purple and White convertible pace car model for sale to the public under option code Z4A—Indy 500 Pace Car Replica. Dealers in the United States got 415 units: 87 went to the Indianapolis festival activities, and 20 were exported. The grand total was 527.

Meanwhile, production of the convertible totaled 4,971, compared to 15,711 coupes. The convertible had a base price of $43,665.

Chevrolet advertised 1995 would be the final year of ZR-1 production with production limited to 448, the same as 1994 and 1993.

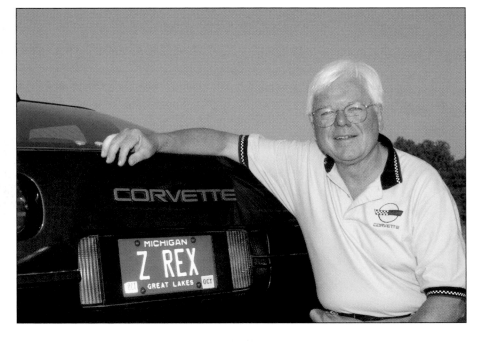

Z-REX

Dave McLellan succeeded Zora Arkus-Duntov as Corvette chief engineer in 1975. The technical highlight of McLellan's tenure with Corvette was the ZR-1, which he called "an important step in the history of the Corvette." Retired today, McLellan drives this 1995 ZR-1 to Corvette shows, where he autographs books and gives seminars.

His personalized Michigan license tags, "Z-REX," have a special meaning. When the ZR-1 was introduced, journalists were treated to a trip to France, all expenses paid by Chevrolet, to drive the dual overhead-cam super car, code named, "King Of The Hill."

"Totally by serendipity we had a number of the cars on Michigan license plates that were three letters and three numbers," McLellan recalled. "Three letters were REX. Rex is Latin for king. So we picked up on that."

1996 CORVETTE GRAND SPORT

In the final year of the fourth-generation Corvette, the ZR-1 was gone and Chevrolet pumped up interest with a couple of one-year-only special editions. The 1996 Grand Sport commemorated the racing Grand Sport of 1963.

RPO Z16 included Admiral Blue paint accented with a white center stripe and two red "hashmarks" on the left front fender. Front brake calipers were finished in special gloss black with the Corvette name in bright aluminum. Wheels were ZR-1 five-spoke versions painted black, but with a 50mm offset rather than 36mm.

The Grand Sport coupe wore ZR-1 tires, requiring unique rear fender flares. Convertible Grand Sport tires were not as wide and did not need the flares.

Exactly 1,000 Grand Sports were built: between 810 coupes and 190 convertibles. All had the new LT4 engine and six-speed manual transmission.

1996 GRAND SPORT REGISTRY

When you look up 1996 Grand Sport in the Corvette dictionary, you'll find John "Hutch" Hutchinson's picture there. Hutch is a typical Corvette enthusiast, very outgoing and friendly. But he goes the extra, extra mile by organizing car shows and Corvette people into one of the best registries in the country.

He owns a Grand Sport coupe; his wife, Patti, owns a Grand Sport convertible. Anything and everything you want to know about the Grand Sport is listed on their web site for the Grand Sport Registry at *http://www.grandsportregistry.com*. And membership is open to all Corvette enthusiasts, not just Grand Sport owners.

1996 COLLECTOR EDITION CONVERTIBLE

Costing a mere $1,250 extra was RPO Z15, known as the "Collector Edition" for 1996. Another one-year wonder, the Collector Edition proved very popular with sales of 5,412, divided between 4,031 coupes and 1,381 convertibles.

The graphics were Sebring Silver paint and the body sported Collector Edition badges. Like the Grand Sport, the Collector Edition used the ZR-1's good-looking, five-spoke wheels, but painted the silver color. Tires were not ZR-1 size, but measured P255/45ZR17 up front and P285/40ZR17 in the rear.

All convertibles came with black soft tops. Interior choices were limited to black, red or gray.

This car is part of the Monty Hall Collection.

1996 LT4 ENGINE

There was no LT5 DOHC V-8 for the last year of the fourth-generation Corvette. Chevrolet produced an optional LT4 with 30 more horsepower than the LT1. Higher compression and new aluminum heads fitted with roller rockers, plus a more aggressive camshaft profile helped the 350-cid LT4 achieve 330 horsepower at 6300 rpm.

LT4 had some great graphics going on under the hood. The new 1996 throttle body featured "Grand Sport" lettering in red.

The LT4 was optional in any 1996 Corvette.

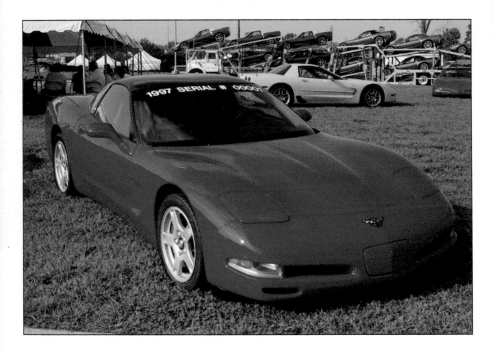

1997 CORVETTE SPORT COUPE

The fifth-generation "C5" Corvette arrived in 1997. There was no convertible the first year.

The car had an all-new chassis and all-new body. Numerous technological advances, including hydro-formed side frame rails, were produced from a single piece of tubular steel.

The transmission was mounted at the rear for improved weight distribution, front to rear.

You can see this car and many other historic Corvettes at the National Corvette Museum in Bowling Green, Kentucky.

The new-generation V-8 debuted with the new C5 models. Old-school Corvette people bemoaned the loss of their beloved "small block" as it was affectionately known.

The new LS1 350 was an entirely new Chevrolet V-8. Engineers stayed with pushrod valves, which still seemed old school. The block featured a Y-block design with cross bolted, four-bolt mains. The intake was a composite that saved weight, and there were other high tech features.

The 350-cid LS1 developed 345 horsepower.

Getting into the seat of a C5 was much easier than climbing into the C4. The "step-over" height was reduced about 3 inches. The seats were also a new design, made by the Lear Corporation. There was a standard seat and optional Sport Seats for an additional $625.

The cockpit was as high-tech as the rest of the car, featuring a console dividing a twin-pod instrument panel. A large tach and speedometer were analog with white pointers on black backgrounds. The emergency brake lever was moved from the driver's left to the console, which also featured a glovebox.

1998 CORVETTE PACE CAR CONVERTIBLE

For 1998, Chevy had the Corvette convertible ready. It also used this body style on the Indianapolis 500 Pace Car replica, featuring a purple exterior with yellow stripes, yellow wheels and an interior in black and yellow.

A total of 1,163 Pace Cars were built at a cost of $5,039 over the base $44,425 price of the convertible.

For the first time since 1962, the convertible came with a separate trunk with outside access.

This example resides in Andy Roderick's "Taj Garage" Collection.

Corvette people like to give their "kids" a nice room, great for entertaining.

1998 LPE, TWIN-TURBO WIDE-BODY CORVETTE COUPE

With a much-improved chassis and power train, C5 Corvettes lent themselves to incredible power levels when modified in the shops of tuners such as Lingenfelter Performance Engineering (LPE), located in Decatur, Indiana.

LPE built this twin-turbo 427 wide-body Corvette coupe.

How fast is this thing? How about a top speed of more than 240 mph, 0-to-60 mph under 3 seconds, and the quarter-mile in 9.36 seconds @ 151.7 mph.

It is a beefed-up automatic—simply floor the gas pedal and hang on. And it's street legal!

This monster, dubbed "Wretched Excess," is owned by Maryland resident Rich Rembold.

1998 CALLAWAY C12 CORVETTE SPEEDSTER

Callaway created a masterpiece starting with a C5 and called it the C12. Low and looking like a racecar, the C12 is one of the world's most desirable super cars.

The custom body is made of fiberglass, carbon fiber and Kevlar. Seen here is the Speedster, featuring a unique rear deck lid with headrests.

The car carried 470 brake horsepower and 450 lbs. ft of torque. Its top speed was listed at 182 mph and it was capable of 12.5-second runs in the quarter-mile.

The larger-than-average size combined with a coach-built body gives the C12 an aggressive look. Like its predecessors, the C12's large twin exhaust system further enhanced its appearance.

1999 CORVETTE HARDTOP

The new hardtop, a third body style, joined the coupe and convertible in 1999, giving the Corvette three body styles for the first time in its history. The hardtop model had a fixed roof and an external trunk lid.

It was a no-frills Corvette, lighter by 80 lbs. than the coupe, and having manual transmission and the Z51 Performance Handling Suspension.

The small back glass identifies this as a hardtop.

Chevy built 4,031 of these cars at a base price of $38,777.

1999 CORVETTE SPORT COUPE

The 1999 coupe and convertible were largely unchanged from 1998. A heads-up display reflected gauges onto the windshield for viewing while the driver was looking at the road ahead.

The 345-hp 350 LT1 was standard. A power telescoping steering column was optional, except on the hardtop.

There were 18,078 coupes and 11,161 convertibles built for the model year. The coupe listed at $39171, while the convertible was $45,579.

Notice the large back window that identifies this as a coupe.

2000 CORVETTE SPORT COUPE

C5 styling remained largely unchanged in the coupe, convertible and hardtop, as Corvettes were available in three body styles for the second straight year.

The passenger-side key cylinder lock was eliminated because Active Keyless entry had become standard. There was a slight change in the standard wheel design. Wheels were also available polished for $895 extra.

Production for the year included 18,113 coupes, 13,479 convertibles and 2,090 hardtops.

CORVETTE C5-R GTS RACE CAR

This is one of the two cars that marked Corvette's return to racing in 1999. It is chassis #002. The C5-R was the first-ever factory designed, built and financed race team in Corvette history. Here, it is seen in the exact configuration last raced at LeMans in 2000.

Pratt and Miller Engineering built and maintained the car. Corvette went racing to improve the breed. In their first appearance at the 24-Hours of Le Mans in June of 2000, the C5-R cars placed third and fourth in the GTS class and 10th and 11th overall.

The first GTS-class victory by a C5-R came at the American LeMans series race in Forth Worth, Texas, with Ron Fellows and Andy Pilgrim driving.

2001 CORVETTE Z06 HARDTOP

2001 marked the debut of the Z06, offered only on the lighter-weight hardtop. All hardtops were Z06s. A new LS6 engine harkened back to the original LS6 454 big-block option code of 1970.

The Z06 cars were easily identified by red brake calipers, stainless-steel mesh in the front grille openings, and scoops just ahead of the rear wheels.

Goodyear Eagle F1 Supercar tires were 1 inch wider and more than 20 lbs. lighter than tires on the coupe and convertible. The windshield and backlite also were made of thinner glass to save weight.

The Z06 awarded "Automobile of the Year" by *Automobile Magazine*.

Production included 15,861 coupes, 14,173 convertibles, and 5,773 Z06 hardtops.

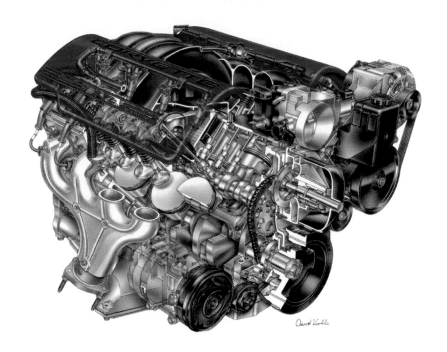

David Kimble

2001 CORVETTE LS6

At the heart of the Z06 was RPO LS6, the 350-cubic inch V-8 based on the LS1. The LS6 is only available with the Z06. It created 385 hp at 6000 rpm and 385 lbs.-ft. of torque at 4800 rpm. The carried unique red fuel rail covers.

These motors featured a new block casting, new intake and exhaust manifolds, higher-flow cylinder heads and fuel injectors, and a more aggressive camshaft profile. Titanium exhaust manifolds saved almost 20 lbs. over the LS1.

2002 CORVETTE Z06 HARDTOP

The LS6 improved by 20 horsepower in 2002, from 385 to 405. The improvement came from new hollow-stem valves, higher-lift camshaft, a low-restriction mass air flow sensor and a new low-restriction air cleaner.

Fender badges below Z06 read "405." This figure matched the top-rated LT5 engine in the early 1990's ZR-1. A heads-up display was made standard on the Z06, and the Second Generation Active Handling system became standard equipment on all Corvettes. Automatic transmission cooler cases were made of lightweight cast aluminum, replacing stainless steel.

The Z06 continued to be based on the hardtop and carried a sticker price of $50,555. The coupe, convertible and hardtop retained their styling from the previous year.

Total Corvette production included 14,760 coupes, 12,710 convertibles, and 8,297 Z06 hardtops.

2002 SKUNK WERKES Z06 CONVERTIBLE

Officially, Chevrolet would not build a Z06 convertible. However, its Skunk Werkes operation did. Henry Iovino is the chief engineer. Chief designer is John Cataro, the styling ace behind the C5 itself. Both Cafaro and Iovino worked within GM's truck division. However, they were key members of the team that designed the C5 and are still Vette people at heart. They continue to work on the car they love in their spare time after work and on assorted weekends.

Skunk Werkes operates in a small shop in the basement of Iovino's house. Chuck Conkle, who is a Pontiac dealer in Kokomo, Indiana, custom ordered this red Z06 convertible, which included the LS6 with 100 more horsepower, body kit, high-rise hood, and a high-tech, exotic interior.

2003 CORVETTE 50TH ANNIVERSARY

The 50th anniversary of the original Corvette was definitely a time to celebrate. Chevrolet had fitted three 2003 coupes for pace car duty, including pacing the May, 2002 Indy 500 race, kicking off the year leading up to the 50th anniversary of the Corvette.

There was no Indy Pace Car replica for the public. Instead, Chevy offered a 50th Anniversary Package on the coupe and convertible (but not the Z06). Option code 1SC included unique Anniversary Red paint, specific badges, unique Shale interior, and chumpagne-painted anniversary wheels with special emblems. All anniversary models came with the new Magnetic Selective Ride Control.

The option package tacked $5,000 onto the price of a new Corvette. The base coupe sold for $43,475, the convertible $50,375 and Z06 hardtop $51,275.

Total production was 16,165 coupes, 12,216 convertibles, and 5,683 Z06 hardtops.

2004 CORVETTE Z06 HARDTOP

The Commemorative Edition Z06 was the top dog in the 2004 lineup. It was also available on coupe and convertible. Commemorating the success of the C5-R racing Corvettes, this special package included LeMans Blue paint, Shale interior, special badges and polished wheels.

Only the Z06 Commemorative Edition came with a red, silver and blue carbon-fiber composite hood, which shaved 10.6 lbs. off the standard hood. Even though a new-generation Corvette, the C6, was due in 2005, the '04 Z06 sold an amazing 5,683 units.

2004 INDY PACE CAR CORVETTE

For the sixth time, a Corvette paced the Indianapolis 500 race. The C5 was virtually ready for the race in street trim.

Minor changes included a heavy-duty transmission, power steering cooler, lower-restriction muffler system, four-point safety belts and the required safety strobe light system. Paint was two-tone white-and-blue incorporating Chevy's new "An American Revolution" marketing theme.

An Indy Pace Car replica was not made available to the public.

2005 CORVETTE SPORT COUPE

The impressive C6 sixth-generation Corvette debuted for 2005, featuring a shorter body and less front overhang. A big change was the fixed headlights, which returned for first time since 1962. The egg-crate grille was reminiscent of 1950s cars.

The cars had a new Keyless Access system with Push Button Start. A new interior had aluminum accents in functional areas like the manual shift knob and door release buttons.

The new LS2 engine was standard. This 6.0-liter V-8 boasted 400 horsepower, highest ever in a small block. It carried the new 'Vette from 0 to 60 mph in 4.1 seconds and quarter-mile in 12.6 @ 114 mph. Top speed was 186 mph.

Here, the new C6 is unveiled at the National Corvette Museum to enthusiasts and the press.

2005 CORVETTE CONVERTIBLE

The 2005 convertible had the same chassis setup as the coupe. The car also had the first power-top option since 1962. A bulkhead was placed in the cargo area to keep things out of the power-top mechanism.

A T56 manual six-speed was standard, and the new 4L65-E Hydra-Matc four-speed automatic was optional

2005 CORVETTE Z06 COUPE

The 2005 Z06 is the fastest street legal production Corvette ever. With a 0-to-60 mph time under 4 seconds, it can do sub-12 second quarter-miles. The LS7 small block engine has 427 cubic inches and supplies 500 horsepower @ 6200 rpm.

Hydro-formed rails are aluminum in the Z06 instead of steel. The engine cradle is lightweight magnesium.

Front fenders and wheelhouses are made of carbon fiber. Floorboards are sheet-carbon.

The cars also featured a lightweight, fixed magnesium roof panel and functional hood scoop, mounted in the center.

Z06 flared fenders are 3 inches wider than the standard C6, with cooling ducts for rear brakes, a specific nose and tail, and unique five-spoke wheels.